EVERYDAY
MAGIC
FOR KIDS

EVERYDAY MAGIC FOR KIDS

30 AMAZING MAGIC TRICKS
That You Can Do Anywhere

JUSTIN FLOM

RP|KIDS
PHILADELPHIA

Running Press Kids
Hachette Book Group
1290 Avenue of the Americas, New York, NY 10104
www.runningpress.com/rpkids
@RP_Kids

Printed in China

First Edition: November 2018

Published by Running Press Kids, an imprint of Perseus Books, LLC,
a subsidiary of Hachette Book Group, Inc. The Running Press Kids name and
logo is a trademark of the Hachette Book Group.

The Hachette Speakers Bureau provides a wide range of authors for speaking events.
To find out more, go to www.hachettespeakersbureau.com or call (866) 376-6591.

The publisher is not responsible for websites (or their content)
that are not owned by the publisher.

Print book cover and interior design by Jason Kayser

Library of Congress Control Number: 2017963214

ISBNs: 978-0-7624-9260-2 (paperback), 978-0-7624-9259-6 (ebook)

1010

10 9 8 7 6 5 4 3 2 1

This book is dedicated to my dad.
I've had many magic heroes, but only one who
watched me when I was terrible and who
patiently shared wisdom on many car rides home
from shows. My dad was the first magician to fool me
and the first to make me laugh. Now I try to do the
same for him with my own magic.

Dad, thank you for showing me the way.

CONTENTS

..... — .....

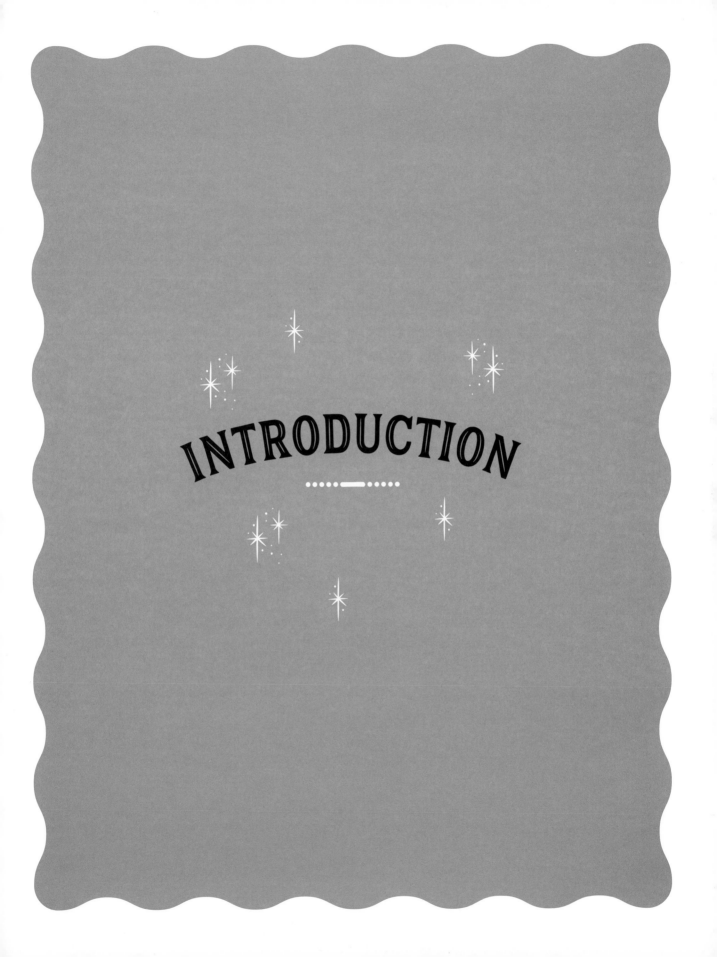

INTRODUCTION

I still have my first magic book from when I was a kid. Well, it wasn't mine exactly; it was my dad's. That's right: I was lucky enough to have a magician for a dad! Growing up, I was surrounded by the coolest and most magical characters you could imagine. Our backyard barbecues were full of fire jugglers, unicyclists, and moms being cut in half. Really! It was as fun and wondrous for a kid as you can imagine.

I fell in love with magic—with searching for secrets, learning the sleights of hand, and performing the impossible. That's why I still cherish my first magic book: *Houdini's Escapes and Magic* by Walter B. Gibson. It is thick as a brick with antique yellowed pages curled with age. It is from the year 1930 and full of stories from vaudeville, which is where Americans first experienced grand magic in the theater. I remember hiding behind my dad's secret passageway (our house had three hidden doors—even my bedroom was behind a moving bookcase!) and studying the magic tricks and classified methods of years past. And that's what started me on my path to becoming a magician.

So welcome to *your* new journey in the world of magic. I am *thrilled* for you. Magic can be a lifelong pursuit or a fun hobby—and it's sure to teach you new things every day. When I was a kid, magic helped me make friends at school, it caught the attention of a girl who eventually married me, and has taken me around the world. But even if this is just a hobby, what you find in this book could change your life for the better.

There are thirty tricks within these pages and all of them have been proven to amaze audiences. Growing up, my audience was usually friends and family, so I've written this book from that perspective. Each trick will begin by explaining how your friend or family member will see the trick, and then I will reveal the secret to the trick and what you need to build or practice. I've always said that magic is more arts and crafts than it is spells and wizardry. And don't get discouraged if you can't do the secret move immediately! Magic is a lifelong pursuit, and the challenge of getting the trick right is part of the fun. I suggest you go through the book in order because I've made sure each new skill and secret builds on the last to help you advance as an aspiring magician.

Ready? Let's make magic and share joy!

EVERYDAY MAGIC
for Kids

the GROCERY GAMBIT

A.K.A. THE PEANUT BUTTER, JELLY, AND PICKLES TRICK

I want to open this book with my favorite trick to teach. I call it the Grocery Gambit, but your friends will call it what it is: amazing!

Your friend is going to make a choice, and you will then reveal that you knew exactly what decision they would make. It's an astounding prediction, and you're right every time! Here is what it looks like if you were to perform it for your friend: You have a jar of peanut butter, a jar of jelly, and a jar of pickles. You say to your friend, "Pick one! The peanut butter, jelly, or pickles, but make sure that it is a free choice. At the end of this, you may think I made you choose one or the other. But no! I want this to be your decision. So, what'll it be?"

Let's say in this example your friend chooses pickles. You reply, "I knew you were going to say pickles. Let me show you how I knew that." And you unscrew the jar of pickles and you show everyone that inside the jar of pickles, written on the lid in magic marker, are the words PICK PICKLES! (1)

But it gets even better. Your audience is kinda impressed, but they still seem skeptical. You then say, "I know what you're thinking. You are thinking that there is a written prediction underneath *all* of the lids. Well, you are right." Then for the fantastic climax you unscrew the lid to the jelly and you show them that the jelly reads PICK PICKLES! Finally, you unscrew the lid of the peanut butter and the peanut butter jar also reads PICK PICKLES! Somehow you knew that your friend was going to pick pickles and you predicted it not once but three times!

Here's the secret to the trick: You are prepared with three different predictions no matter what your friend chooses. If they pick pickles, you reveal your prediction underneath the lid of the jar. But you have two other hidden predictions. You have jelly written on the back of each of the jars and you have peanut butter written underneath each of the jars. Pretty sneaky. This relies on the fact that the audience doesn't know how the trick ends; they're just told to make a choice.

I made my peanut butter, jelly, and pickles jars with labels from the store. You can also use paper, scissors, and glue. You'll need three of each prediction totaling nine labels. Three will be hidden in the lid, three underneath the jars, and three at the back (2).

Once you have made your specially prepared jars, you are ready to do the trick. You display the jars with the audience standing in front of you. (Note: This is a trick in which the audience cannot stand behind you or they will see your hidden predictions on the back of the jars.) You tell them to make a selection, but make sure that it is a free choice. Let's say they choose jelly. Then you say, "I want to show you that I knew you were going to pick jelly because I wrote down a prediction on the back of one of these jars." And you reveal on the back of the jelly jar that it reads PICK JELLY!

Now you let your audience be impressed but skeptical and that is when you can reveal the rest of the trick by saying, "I know what you are thinking. There is writing on the back of all of the jars. Well, you are right." And then you reveal that all of the jars read PICK JELLY on the back.

The same goes if your friend picks peanut butter and you reveal the bottom of the jars. The important thing to remember as you reveal the jar's back or bottom, or under the lid, is to be careful not to reveal your other hidden predictions. This is an amazing trick that you can do in your kitchen at home or onstage for a bigger audience. And if you don't have peanut butter, jelly, or pickles in your house, you can use any food or items that have three different options for predictions. Be creative and create your own Grocery Gambit!

2

DOLLAR DESTRUCTION

This is an incredible piece of magic where you can borrow a dollar bill from your friend, destroy part of it (even eat it), and still put the dollar back together. It is a really cool trick. The secret is in the way that you tear the dollar bill and make it look like you ate a piece of it.

Here is what you do: Borrow a dollar bill from your friend and fold that bill in half. Now, you are going to make a tear at one side, but you are not going to tear off the piece completely. You are going to go about a half inch from the side of the dollar bill and rip down about half an inch. The audience can see that you really are tearing the bill (1).

Now, in one final grasp and rip, you are actually going to fold that piece of the dollar bill behind the bill, so the audience can't see it, and you hold that with your left thumb. Along with that move, you make it look like you jerk your fingers away from the bill and that you have ripped off the piece (2). You immediately mime like you are putting that in your mouth.

To the audience it looks like you have chewed up the dollar bill (and maybe like you have even swallowed it). It's time for you to create the illusion that you have spit the piece back to the dollar bill and that it is whole again. Your left hand is still holding the dollar bill with the piece folded behind it. With your right hand, put your fingers inside of the bill, holding on to the right side of the bill. Your left hand now readjusts and grabs the other side of the bill (the left side of the bill) but doesn't yet open it.

For dramatic effect, make it sound like you are spitting the piece of the bill back up and onto the folded bill. When you do that, you are going to quickly open the bill, making sure it's taut by spreading your left and right hands. The corner folded behind the bill will jump back into place and make it appear as though the dollar is whole again (3).

As long as you hold the bill tight, the tear will look like it is completely healed. At this point, I usually say, "Thanks so much for your dollar bill." And I put it in my pocket. Now your friend is going to ask for his dollar bill back. At this point, I take out a different dollar bill and I give it back to him. The different dollar bill that I have given back to him does not have the tear in it. Your friend can inspect that bill to his heart's content, sure that you've just ate it and then reattached part of the bill.

But what do you do with your dollar bill that has the tear in it? It is actually okay to spend money if it has a little bit of a tear. You can put some tape over that part and then spend it on anything you like.

JUMPING
RUBBER BANDS

This is the very first trick that I started performing for my friends when I was a kid. Really, this is an amazing trick and it has stood the test of time. It will look as though rubber bands can jump between your fingers in a blink of an eye.

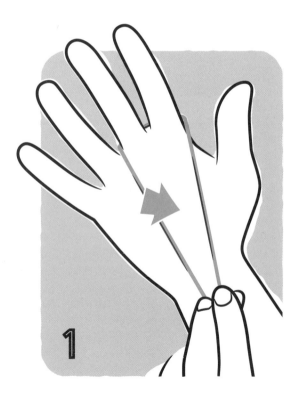

Here's how you do the trick: Take a rubber band and put it on your first two fingers (your index finger and your middle finger). This is the first position, and this is where the trick begins. Now, grab the rubber band with your palm facing you and stretch it out so that you can fit your four fingers inside the space created by the stretched rubber band (1). Close your four fingers and slowly and secretly rest the outstretched rubber band on the back of your fingernails (2).

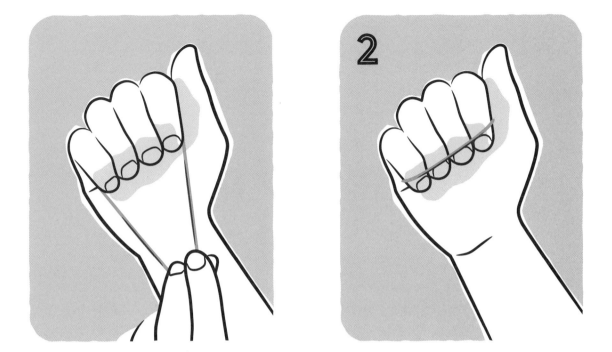

Now when you open your fist, the magic will happen automatically, and the rubber band will appear to jump to your other two fingers (your ring finger and your pinkie). Keep in mind that you can do this again in reverse by stretching the rubber band out and placing your four fingers in again, resting the rubber band on your fingernails, and opening your fist, but you want to try to make the movement of closing your fingers inside the rubber band a secret. I like to do it like I'm adjusting the rubber band as I close my fist, when in reality, I have closed those four fingers into the gap and secretly rested the rubber band on the back of my fingernails.

And that is how you make a rubber band jump instantly between your fingers!

Locked JUMPING RUBBER BANDS

If you thought the previous trick was pretty cool, then you are about to make it even more amazing! What if you could lock that rubber band from trick #3 in place but still be able to make it jump and change locations? You can do this by locking a rubber band around your fingers. And believe it or not, the trick works exactly the same as in #3.

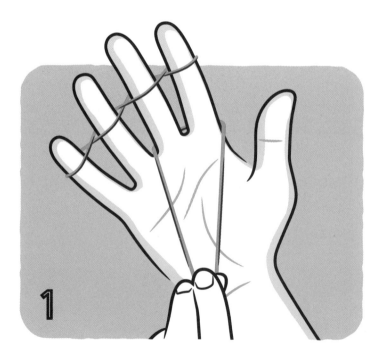

1

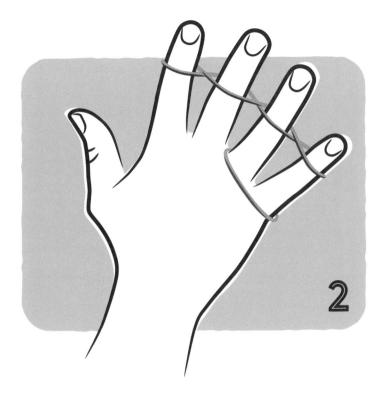

Put the rubber band on your index and middle fingers and take a second rubber band and twist it around each finger like a figure 8, creating a cage above the first rubber band. Now, you perform the trick exactly as you learned before. Stretch the rubber band that is on your first two fingers back toward you (1), close your fingers into a fist, rest the rubber band on your fingernails, and now when you open your hand, even despite being locked in place, the rubber band jumps to your fourth and fifth fingers (2)!

I don't know about you, but I do this trick in the mirror for myself sometimes, just because it seems like real magic. I am still amazed by it.

AMAZING
Paper Clip

Sometimes in magic, you can use similar methods for a completely different effect. In the last two tricks, you have been making a rubber band teleport fingers using one specific method. But now you are going to use that same method for a totally different trick. In fact, if you do it right, your audience won't think the rubber bands move at all because now you are making a paper clip teleport across the rubber bands!

This is like a close-up linking rings trick, one of the oldest tricks in magic. But it uses ordinary objects (some rubber bands and a paper clip) instead of rings, and it is far more visual because the paper clip will instantly unlink from one rubber band and onto the other rubber band all while in the spectator's hands. They never let go of the paper clip, and the magic happens right at their fingertips.

Here's how the trick works:
You start with two rubber bands on
your hand: one on your index finger
and middle finger, and the second
rubber band on your ring finger and
pinkie. You give your friend a paper clip
and tell them to link it onto one of the
rubber bands. They can choose any
one they like (1). For example, if they
put the paper clip on the rubber band
around your pinkie and ring finger, you
are going to make that paper clip
unlink and link onto the other rubber
band. Here's how you do it:

First, you grab the rubber band
that the paper clip is not linked to and
you stretch it back the same as in the
position of the jumping rubber bands.
Next, you grab the rubber band on
your ring and pinkie fingers, which is
underneath the other rubber band. It is
important to make sure that the rubber
band without the paper clip is the
rubber band on top (2).

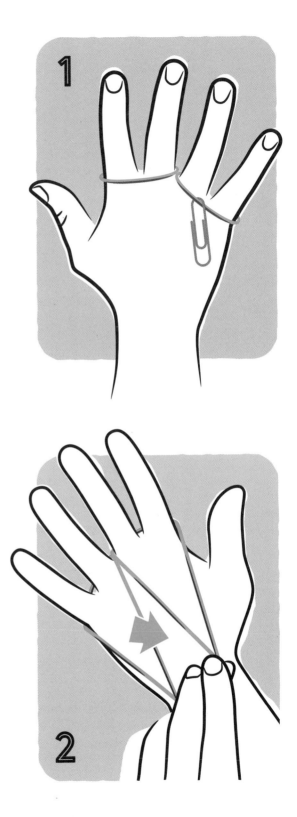

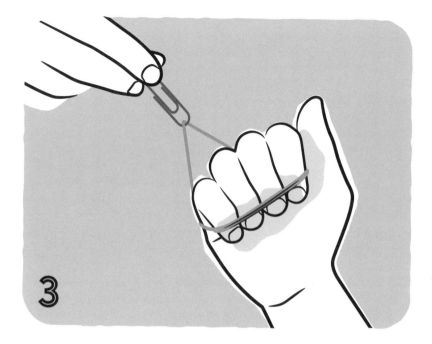

Now, you will see that three triangles have been created by outstretching the rubber bands. You want to place your four fingers, as you did in the jumping rubber bands trick, inside the middle triangle, and then you rest both rubber bands on the back of your fingernails (3). What is about to happen is that both rubber bands will switch places and the paper clip will go along for the ride. However, to the spectator, it is going to look like the paper clip instantly unlinks and links onto the adjacent rubber band. All you have to do is open your fist.

What I like to do with this trick is have the spectator hold on to the paper clip the whole time and even wiggle it around a little bit as I open my fist. That will help the rubber bands make the trip and will hide the fact that they are actually switching places.

I am really excited about this trick because it is a brand-new version of the jumping rubber bands that adds a whole new visual element and happens in the spectator's hands, making it all the more believable to the audience.

TRICK

#6

COLOR Vision

Want to read someone's mind? Then Color Vision is the trick for you! You are going to make it look like you know exactly what color your friend is thinking of. This is a cool piece of mind-reading magic.

Here is what the trick looks like to your friend: You have five crayons, and you hold them behind your back as you turn away from your friend. You tell your friend to take all of the crayons and to pick one (1). Whichever one they pick, put it back in your hands behind your back. And now your friend hides the rest of the crayons. You turn around to make your miraculous revelation. You hold your hand out in front of you. You think hard and you reveal exactly what they are thinking. "You chose the color blue," you say to your friend. And you were right!

How did you do it? Well, it's a little piece of sneaky subterfuge. When your friend puts the crayon that they are thinking of behind your back, you scratch off a piece of that wax Crayola crayon using your fingernail of your thumb (2). Now, when you turn back around and look them in the eye, you make a mysterious motion with your hand. What you are actually doing is looking right at that chunk of crayon stuck in your thumbnail that the audience can't see (3). Now, you can see clearly from the residue of the crayon in your thumbnail that your friend chose a particular color.

But you should definitely remember to make a bit of a show of it. You can say, "I believe you are thinking of the color red." And then you can bring your other hand from around your back and reveal, yep, there it is—the red crayon. This is another trick that you can even do twice or maybe three times because the method is so clever.

SPOON BEND

Bending a spoon is a classic magician's trick, but what do you do with a bent spoon? Wouldn't it be cool if you could make it look like a spoon can bend and snap back into its original state instantly? With this spoon-bending trick, you can do just that. I still perform this trick when I'm out at a restaurant or at a friend's house for dinner. All you need is a spoon and your hands.

Here is what the audience sees: You are going to grunt as you bend a spoon against your friend's table and then instantly reveal that the spoon is back to normal.

Here's how it works: It is a stunning illusion that relies on a little sleight of hand. You have to hold the spoon in your right hand so it is laid across your first three fingers, but your pinkie is laid on top of that spoon (1).

Now, place the bowl of the spoon against the table (2) and then you are going to rotate your right hand forward, allowing the spoon to pivot between your pinkie and ring finger. As you rotate your hand forward (3), both your thumbs let go of the stem of the spoon at the top so that the spoon drops down flat against the table (4). The audience can still see the bowl of the spoon, so as your hands bend forward, it gives the illusion that you're bending the spoon against the table. This illusion works because your empty hands appear to be gripping the stem of the spoon.

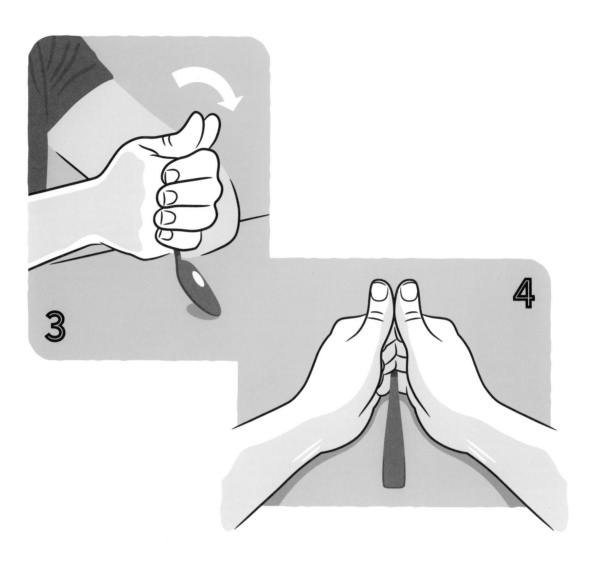

When all of these actions are done together, it looks like the spoon bends almost in half. But instantly you can restore the spoon back to its original state by pressing down with your left hand on the bowl of the spoon and lifting up with your the pinkie of your right hand to bring the stem of the spoon back into your left fingers. Now, you spread your hands to reveal the spoon is still intact.

Spoon VANISHED

Once you know how to bend a spoon, you can also work on making a spoon vanish into thin air! With this trick, you'll make it look like you've made a spoon completely disappear.

The secret is in your lap. What does this mean? It means you are going to very secretly get the spoon from the table to your lap without the audience knowing. In magic, this is a term called *lapping*.

Here's how it works: The spoon is on the table in front of you, placed sideways so that you can cover it up with your left and right hand, touching each other at the fingertips and covering the spoon (1). It is going to look like you are dragging the spoon off the table into your hands, holding it in the air about a foot above the table.

In reality, though, you are going to drag that spoon and you won't grab it at all. You will let it freely fall into your lap as you lift your hands up (2), pretending that you still have the spoon. The key is to be completely fluid in your motion—your hands come down, cover the spoon, and drag it off the table up into the air while you are actually allowing the spoon to fall into your lap.

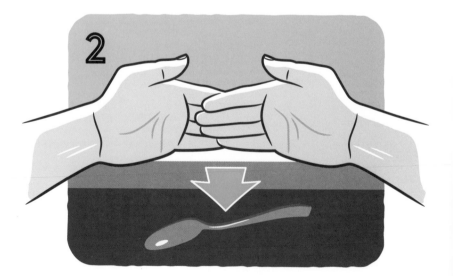

Now, you wait about three seconds for time misdirection. *Time misdirection* is when the audience forgets a moment that just happened. In this case, the audience will forget that your hands were close to the edge of the table. And now you make it look like you are bending the spoon in the air once again and then instantly open all of your fingers, open your hands, and reveal that the spoon is gone (3).

Sometimes I will have a magician buddy sitting next to me who will take the spoon out of my lap and put it in another friend's purse or maybe pull it out of his pocket to make it look like the spoon disappeared and went there. Either way, it is a really fun trick that I know you will love performing time and again for your friends.

SALT SHAKER VANISHED

Recently when I performed on television, I had the opportunity to do an amazing piece of magic and I chose to do this trick because I believe it's *that* good. You are lucky because I'm about to tell you the secret so you, too, can perform this amazing trick anytime or anyplace.

The audience is going to see you make a salt shaker completely disappear right under your friend's hand. To do this trick, all you need is a napkin, a salt shaker, and a quarter or other kind of coin (1). The coin is for misdirection only. The audience will be looking at the coin at a key moment when you are going to be able to secretly ditch the salt shaker, and that's how it disappears.

Here's how it happens: You tell the audience that you are going to do the amazing quarter (or coin) vanish trick. Begin by placing the coin on the table. "We need a shroud of mystery. We will use this salt shaker and this napkin," you say as you put the napkin over the salt shaker (2).

Here's the secret to the trick: The napkin will hold the form
of the salt shaker even if the salt shaker isn't under the napkin.
If you combine that secret with what we learned recently about
lapping (taking something off the table and ditching it in your lap),
then you can make the salt shaker disappear as if by magic.

So, you have the quarter on the table and the salt shaker
underneath the napkin. You say, "Watch the quarter. We are
going to make it disappear." And you cover it with the salt shaker
under the napkin. You snap your fingers or say a magic word
and bring your hand back, revealing that the coin hasn't disappeared at all. It is still there.

At this point you say, "Oh, I forgot. It is very important that the coin be heads up." Or it can be the reverse if you like. This is not important to the magic trick, but important that the audience have their eyes on the coin because it is at this exact moment that your left hand, which is holding the salt shaker, comes back to the edge of the table and you loosen your grip on the salt shaker so that it falls from the napkin into your lap. But notice that the napkin still retains the shape of the salt shaker (3).

Now, you go back to cover up the coin once again to make it disappear. The audience believes the salt shaker is still there because they see the form of the salt shaker in the napkin, but it is already gone. Have your friend put their hand over and above the salt shaker and you take your free hand (your right hand) and smash their hand down on top of the now empty napkin (4). It will feel like the salt shaker disappeared right from under their hand. Say, "Well, I guess we didn't make the coin disappear, but the salt shaker has completely vanished."

It is an *amazing* trick. There are a couple fun things you can do with this trick if you have a buddy who is also a magician. If he is sitting next to you at the table, he can take the salt shaker out of your lap and move it to the other side of the table. Or perhaps she can load it in your friend's bag or even bring it all the way home with him and make it appear someplace really crazy.

Sometimes when I perform this effect, I immediately reappear the salt shaker as if it passed through the table. In order to do that, all I have to do is bring the salt shaker up from my lap and say, "It didn't disappear. It just went right through the table." That is, if I think that I'm going to get caught with the salt shaker in my lap. But most times, I make the salt shaker disappear and I never bring it back. It will drive your friends crazy not knowing how the salt shaker disappeared.

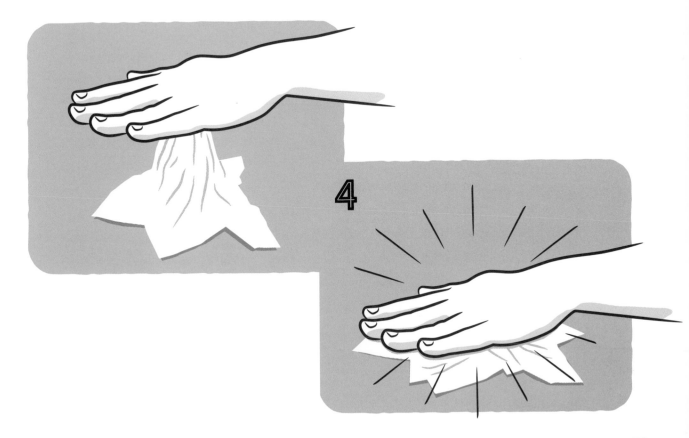

KNIFE from ROLL

H ere is the last amazing feat of magic that you can perform for your friends when you're out eating in a restaurant. It is going to look like you can take a bread roll and pull a knife straight from the inside. This trick drives the waiters and waitresses crazy because it looks like they baked their silverware right inside the bread.

The secret to this trick is simple. With a little preparation you, too, will be able to pull a butter knife from a bread roll. The secret is in your wrist, or really, what you have *around* your wrist.

All you need is a watch or a bracelet or even some rubber bands to hold the butter knife to your left wrist, hidden behind your hand and wrist (1). When you are ready to do the trick, you pick up a roll with your left hand (2). With your right hand, you are going to reach through the roll and grab the knife (3), which is resting in your palm. As you pull it out, it will look like the knife is coming from the center of the roll (4). Once the knife is almost all the way out of the roll and nothing is hidden by your hand, rotate your hand around so they can see your empty palm. It will really look like the knife came from nowhere!

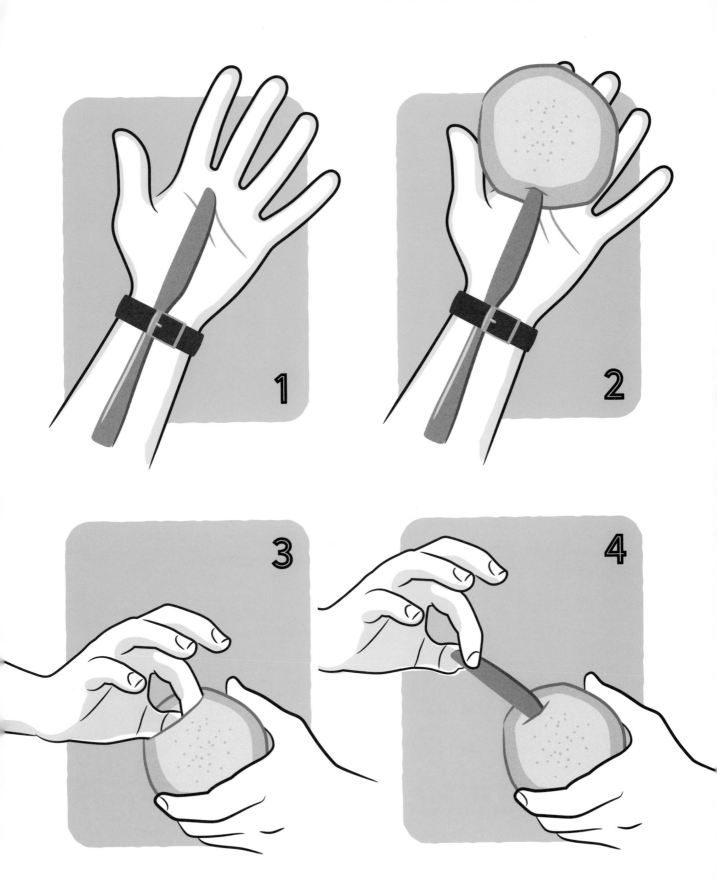

When I perform this effect, I usually keep the knife and roll ready for when the waiter comes to the table. So, instead of grabbing a roll and reaching all the way through the roll to my palm, I have the knife already sticking inside the roll about an inch. But this is hidden because the back of my hand is facing everyone else at the table who is my audience. When I'm ready, I can stick my fingers into the top of the roll and grab that one-inch tip of the knife and pull it all the way through.

This trick works best with a butter knife. Any sort of knife that has a big handle, like a steak knife, will be very difficult to pull through the bread roll (plus, a butter knife has a duller edge so you are less likely to get hurt!). So, it is best to do this with a butter knife, and the longer the butter knife, the more impressive a trick this is.

Mad Money $TAB

Use your money-healing magic to stab a pencil through some cold hard cash and then seal the wound to leave the dollar bill unharmed. Sounds like a cool trick, doesn't it? I'm going to show you the secret to healing a stab wound in George Washington's head (at least the money version of his head).

What your friends will see is that you can stab a pencil through the center of a dollar bill and heal the hole anytime you like. This trick just requires thirty seconds of preparation. There is a hole hidden inside the bill, but it is where your audience would least expect it. It is not where they think the pencil stabs through the bill, but rather it is in a hidden spot within the design of the dollar bill (1).

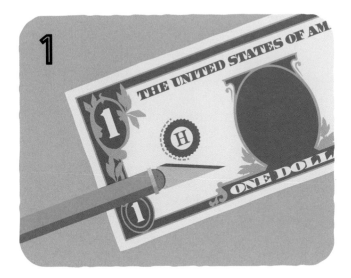

Here's how you prepare your bill: Take an X-Acto knife, a razor blade, or a pair of scissors and cut along the border of the seal in the dollar bill (or ask an adult to help you with the X-Acto knife or razor blade). Now you are ready to perform the effect.

Use a dollar bill and a Post-it note or another piece of small paper. You are going to fold the dollar bill almost in half, but you are going to leave a quarter inch of the side where the cut is exposed (2). This way the audience can see that the pencil is really going inside the fold of the bill and is not hidden behind the bill. As the pencil goes into the fold of the bill, you are actually putting the pencil through that secret hole (3). Now the pencil is underneath the bottom of the bill, but it is still going to stab through the Post-it note that you have folded over the front of the bill (4).

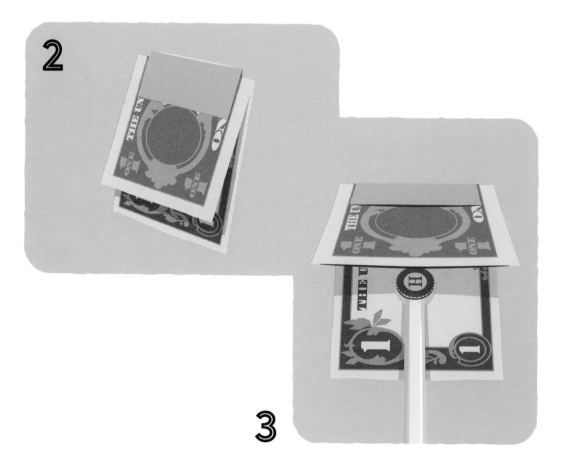

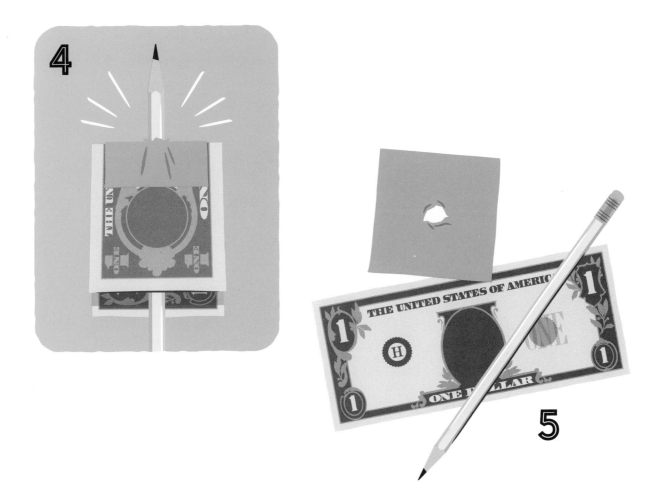

Now it sounds and looks as though the pencil has stabbed through the center of George Washington's head. The audience can see that the pencil is really inside the bill, but when you pull it out and unfold the dollar, George Washington and the bill are completely unharmed (5).

If you are nervous about the audience seeing the hole where the pencil goes through on the seal of the dollar bill, you can cover that up with your thumb when you show the audience. However, I've found that if you use a very fine scissors or knife when cutting the secret hole, it is completely undetectable to the naked eye.

Now let's get stabbing (dollar bills only, of course)!

ROLL
of the DICE

A *coincidence* is something that happens by chance but seems so impossible it is like magic. We are going to create a crazy coincidence with a roll of a dice and a little bit of candy.

It is going to look like this to your friends: They will shake a glass full of dice until they get a random number. Then you pull out your hand and show that you had exactly that amount of jelly beans in your hand the whole time.

How do you predict exactly the amount that your friend rolls on the dice? Easy! You rig the dice to roll the same number every time. It is a really cool method that will fool your friends into thinking that you have the ability to create crazy coincidences.

Here's how it works: In order to do this, you need four or six dice. You are going to glue the dice together in pairs so that four of the sides of each glued pair add up to seven. This is an amazing bit of math and a deception that will fly right by your friends.

On my first set of dice, I glue the *six* to the *one* so that looking directly at me is a *five* and a *two* (1, 2). Then I can rotate the dice around and see that each of the sides next to the glued side adds up to seven. If I were to look at the farthest side of the dice away from each other, those, too, will add up to seven. I do that to two pairs of dice so that now, no matter what a friend rolls, it will always equal fourteen. If I wanted to do it with three pairs of dice, then the total would always be twenty-one.

Decide now if you want to glue two or three pairs of dice. Three is a nice number if you can have a glass that it fits in because you really can't tell that the dice are stuck together when there are that many dice in the glass. Pictured here is a small glass bowl I use to fit three pairs of dice.

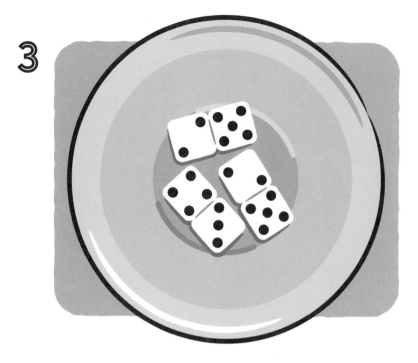

When I use three pairs of dice, I make sure I have twenty-one jelly beans hidden in my hand or in a bag or in a bowl covered up with a cloth and maybe labeled with a piece of paper that says, PREDICTION.

Now I have my friend take their hand and cover up the glass with the dice, shaking it up as much as they want. When they are satisfied, they stop and they peek in and add up all of the numbers that are staring at them (3). When they do that, they will find that the total number is twenty-one (or fourteen if you are only using two pairs of dice).

Unveil your prediction of jelly beans to show them that you have created a crazy coincidence.

Melting MATCHSTICKS

My favorite kind of magic are tricks that are highly visual when an amazing thing happens. I am going to show you how you can make two wooden matchsticks pass through each other like hot knives *melting* through butter.

To do this trick all you need is thick wooden matchsticks, the kind that maybe your parents keep in the kitchen in a big matchbox. Get their permission first to gather two matchsticks to do this amazing trick.

Here's the preparation: The matchstick in your right hand is going to stick to your first finger. How does it stick to your first finger? The chemicals on the top of a matchstick want to stick to your skin when the proper amount of pressure is applied. So, put the first matchstick between your thumb and first finger of your right hand with the matchstick head touching your first finger (1). Press down with a good amount of pressure and after a few seconds you will be able to lift up your first finger and the matchstick will have stuck to it. We can call that "open position" (2).

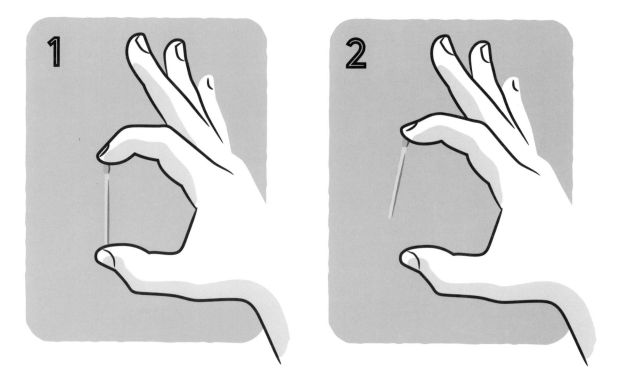

Bring your first finger back down so the matchstick is touching both your thumb and first finger. That's called the closed position. Now you are ready to perform the trick.

Take a matchstick in both hands, holding it between your first finger and thumb. The matchstick in your right hand is ready to be in the open position because you have put pressure on the matchstick head, so it is sticking to that first finger. Be sure not to let the audience see that the matchstick can stick to your skin.

Tell the audience that there is no way to pass wooden matchsticks through each other because they are solid objects. And then in one swoop, bring the matchsticks toward each other and in that motion, go from closed position to open position and let your left hand's matchstick pass right through the opening as you bring your first finger of your right hand back down into closed position (3, 4). When this is done at speed, the matchsticks will look like they passed right through each other by magic.

To undo the illusion, perform the same actions in reverse. With one fluid motion, your right hand goes from closed position to open position and the matchsticks will pass through each other to become unlinked. At that point, I take off the match that is stuck on my first finger and I set both matchsticks on the table so everything can be examined. Your friends will see that there is no trickery to be found with the matchsticks and they'll be super impressed by what you've just done.

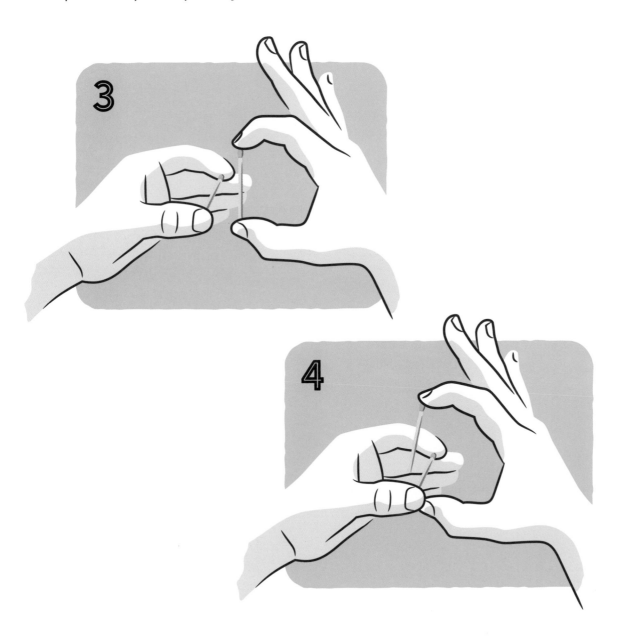

INDESTRUCTIBLE TOOTHPICK

Wouldn't it be magical if you could take something broken and make it go back together to be completely restored? We will be able to do that with a toothpick in this magic trick. Your friends will actually feel and hear the wooden toothpick break, but then you will reveal that it is indestructible and not broken at all.

Here's how to do it: You have a hidden toothpick in the hem of your T-shirt. So before you perform the trick, find a T-shirt that has a hem at the bottom of it and one that you would be okay putting a small hole in. Take a wooden toothpick and hide it in the hem of your T-shirt (1). Now you are ready to perform the trick.

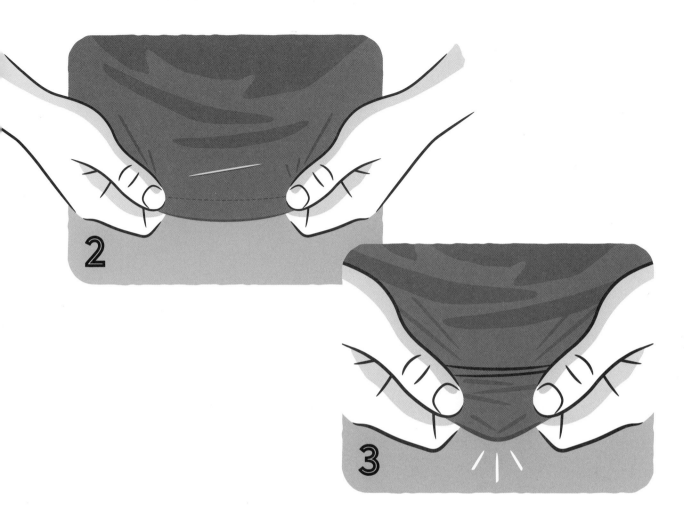

Bring out a box of toothpicks or borrow a toothpick from a restaurant and put it in your shirt like it is a hammock (2). Your friends will see that the toothpick is resting in the bottom of your shirt. You fold your shirt over once, twice, three times, wrapping that toothpick inside your shirt, when really you have kept track of the toothpick hidden in the hem of your shirt. Now you let your friend grab that hidden toothpick, feel it in your shirt, and crack it in half (3). They will swear they heard and felt the toothpick break, and they did! But they broke the *hidden* toothpick so when you unroll your shirt, your friends will see that the toothpick is completely unharmed. Later, when the audience is no longer around, you can remove the hidden, broken toothpick from the hem of your shirt.

TRICK #15

My Precious

A.K.A. VANISHING COIN UNDER A RING OR GLASS

You will soon have the power of invisibility through a ring. This trick is called My Precious because when you put something in the magic rings, it will look invisible. It is a very cool way to make coins magically appear.

A little bit of arts and crafts are required for the making of this trick. All you need are two Styrofoam cups, some pieces of printer paper, scissors, a coin, a playing card, and glue.

Start out by creating your My Precious invisibility rings. These rings are actually the top lip of Styrofoam cups (1). I found that those are easy to make and also very lightweight and fun to play with. To do this, use a pair of scissors and cut into each Styrofoam cup, cutting off the top until you have two rings.

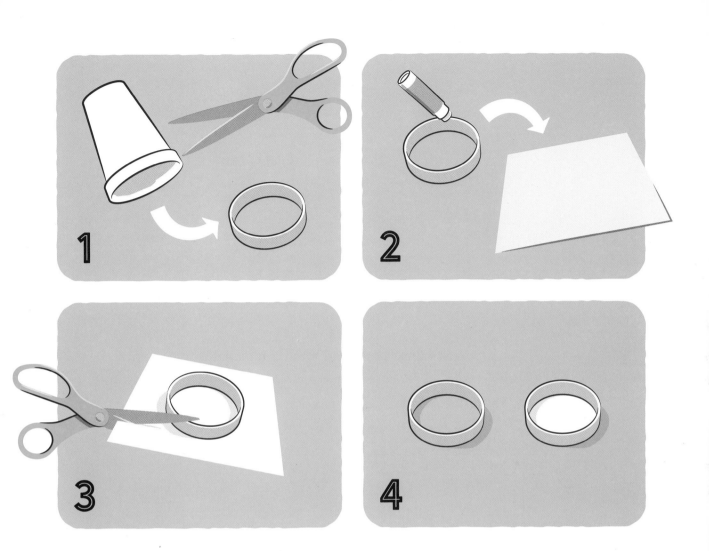

One of these rings will be your secret magic gimmick. The magic gimmick ring has paper glued to the bottom of it. This will help make things invisible! So grab a scrap of paper and glue it to the ring, making sure the paper covers the entire mouth (2). Glue it down onto the mouth of the Styrofoam cup ring using a glue stick. Glue it down firmly, then allow it to dry for just a few minutes and take your scissors and cut around the excess paper so you are left with a Styrofoam cup ring with a paper that is exactly as big as its opening (3, 4).

Now you can place the ring on another piece of printer paper and no one would have any idea that there is paper glued to the bottom of the ring. This will be your invisibility ring and will perfectly hide anything flat that goes underneath it. You are ready to begin the trick.

Start with the coin on the right side of the paper and the invisibility ring over the top of it. The other ring, which you can see through, is to your left. You talk about how in *The Hobbit*, Bilbo Baggins has a special ring that makes him invisible. You can say that you have the same thing here. In fact, if you remove the rings, you will find that there was something sitting there all along (5).

You should take the playing card and place it on the ring on your right, grab the ring on your left, and stack it on top of that (6). Then snap your fingers and move everything to your left. A coin will magically appear (7). If you would like, you can now place the ring around the coin and you will be able to see through that ring, which adds to the deception that one of the rings is one that you can't see through. Or if you prefer to keep the mystery going and say that this ring makes things invisible, then don't place it over the quarter, otherwise it will become invisible.

Now you can repeat the effect to make the coin disappear by doing everything in reverse. Place the card on the Styrofoam ring the farthest to your left. Place the Styrofoam ring without the paper on top of that. Place everything on top of the coin, and it will be gone once again.

This is a very cool way to use ordinary objects around the house to make a coin disappear in an instant.

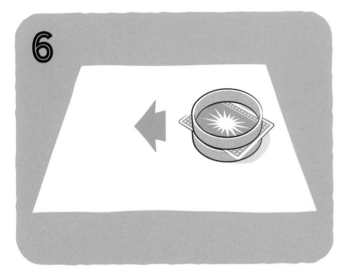

Ace  SWINDLE

An *optical illusion* is something that looks like it actually isn't. Maybe it is something that looks possible when it is impossible, or maybe it is something that you swear you see but it isn't even there. I know it sounds confusing, so let me explain.

We are going to do the Ace Swindle, where your friends will swear that they are holding on to the ace of diamonds when actually the ace of diamonds is nowhere to be found. Some people call this Three-Card Monte, but I call this a whole lot of fun.

You are going to spread your cards in a certain way, and you are going to tell the audience that you have the two black aces and the ace of diamonds. In actuality, you are hiding the ace of hearts in a way that the pointy bottom of the heart looks like a diamond. It is this optical illusion that convinces the audience that they know exactly where the ace of diamonds is when really the ace of diamonds is still inside the deck of cards or in your pocket or maybe even hanging on the wall behind them.

Set up the cards like the picture you see here (1) and say, "I want you to keep track of the ace of diamonds. We have the clubs, the spades, but the ace of diamonds is the important one. I am going to turn the cards facedown, and I will give them a little bit of a mix." At this point, you just deal those cards onto the table and switch two of them. But do this very slowly and fairly so the audience is convinced that they know where the ace of diamonds is.

Now you say, "Where do you think the ace of diamonds is?" When they point to the ace of hearts (which they *think* is the ace of diamonds) you can say, "No, I'm sorry, that the ace of hearts (2). These are the black aces." And then you can reveal that the ace of diamonds is actually on the wall behind them or in your pocket or still in the deck of cards.

That is a real swindle!

CUT ✂ THE SHOESTRING *and* RESTORE

Sawing a lady in half is perhaps the most famous and well-known magic trick of all time. Well, growing up, I didn't have any ladies to saw in half, but I did have my shoestrings. So now I'm going to teach you how to cut your shoestring in half and then put it back together by magic.

To do this effect, all you need is a shoestring, which will be your "lady," and a straw, which will be your sawing-in-half box. It is going to look to your friends like you can put the shoestring through the straw, cut the straw and the string in half, and yet, the string remains completely intact or restored.

Here is a little bit of preparation that you might need help from an adult for because you are going to cut a small incision in the straw. Right in the center, there will be a cut about two inches in length down the center of the straw (1). This is something that needs a knife or an X-Acto blade in order to do, so it is best to ask an adult for help. Once that is done, you are ready to perform the trick.

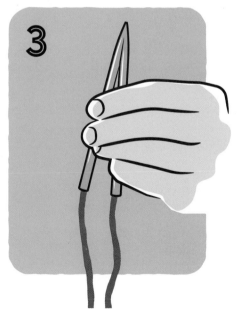

Talk to your audience about sawing a lady in half and tell them that instead of a lady you will use a shoestring. This is an effect where you could even borrow a shoestring from a friend or family member in the crowd. You put the shoestring through the straw (2). It is important to note that the straw should be a solid color, not transparent so that you can see through. Once the shoestring is all the way through the straw, you fold the straw in half (3).

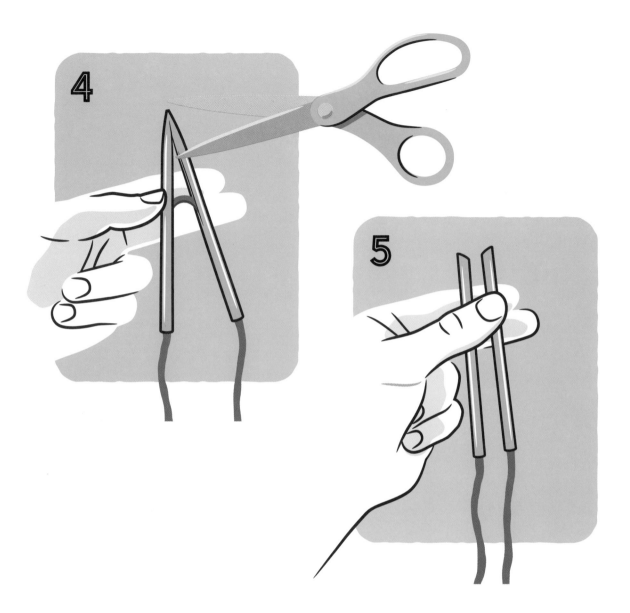

Now, here's the secret move. While holding the folded straw in your fist, you give a tight tug on both loose shoestrings at the bottom of your fist. Doing so will pull the shoestring through the slit and hide it in your hand behind your fingers. Now, you have the perfect spot to open up your hand, covering with just a few fingers where the string is going through the straw (4), and cut above that in the straw. When you cut through the straw, there is no string there, but it will appear to the audience as though you have cut right through the shoestring and the straw (5).

To make the restoration happen, take the straw that is on your right and rotate it around so that it is facing the opposite direction and close both straws in your left fist (6). Now, with one swoop tug, you can pull the shoestring all the way out of both straws and it will miraculously restore.

Now the straws are seen to the audience as trash, so you can throw those away. What they really want to inspect is the string, so hand it over because they can look to their heart's content. There is nothing to see. The magic is done and your secret remains safely hidden in the discarded straw.

TRICK #18

Superhero HAT TRICK

There have always been mysterious stories about individuals who can see through their fingertips, as if the tips of their fingers have extra eyeballs. Now all of those claims are fake and phony—just magic tricks—but I am going to teach you a trick that will make it look like you have eyeballs at your fingertips and that you can read just using the tips of your fingers.

Tell your friends you are going to play a game. You have taken a ton of small pieces of paper and written different superhero names on them (1), and you also have a hat. Have your friends check that all of the papers are different, fold them up, and put them in the hat.

1

WONDER WOMAN
FLASH
AQUAMAN
SUPERMAN
CATWOMAN
ANT MAN
IRON MAN
STORM
BATMAN
THOR
HULK
WOLVERINE
BLACK PANTHER
CAPTAIN AMERICA

Now, as one friend holds the hat high over your head, you reach in and feel around. You grab a piece of paper and apparently read it with the tips of your fingers and announce, "I think I have Superman." Then you take it out and you peek at the paper. You are correct, and you instantly go back into the hat and take another one and say, "Now I think I have Wonder Woman." You take it out, you are correct again, and you show your friends both pieces of paper. You were absolutely right. You *did* read with your fingertips both Superman and Wonder Woman's names. So, how do you do it?

There is a little bit of secret preparation needed for this trick. Before you start, you must take the piece of paper that reads SUPERMAN and fold it up and put it in the lip of fabric underneath the hat (2). Every baseball hat has a lip of fabric that folds up and you can hide things in it. In fact, you can hide this secret piece of paper that reads SUPERMAN in your hat all day until you are ready to perform the trick.

Once you are ready to perform the trick, the Superman piece of paper is hidden in the hat and the different superhero pieces of paper are introduced and checked out by the audience. They can see that they are all different and that they are put into the hat. But how do you magically read the piece of paper with your fingertips twice?

It is a principle in magic called "One Ahead." What you are going to do is the first time you reach in the hat, you take out any piece of paper and it really it is a completely random choice. As you are grabbing that paper you announce, "I believe I have Superman." You take out that paper, and very carefully, so that no one else can see it, open it up for yourself. Now let's say you received Wonder Woman, then you remember Wonder Woman but say, "Yep, I was right. In fact, I'm going to do it again." Now you are "One Ahead" because you're secretly remembering Wonder Woman.

As you reach into the hat a second time, you pull out your secret Superman paper from the lip of fabric (3). With the Superman paper in your fingers, announce: "I believe I have Wonder Woman" (or whichever paper you're remembering from a moment ago). You pull it out and you read it to yourself, careful not to let anyone else see, and you say, "Yep, I was right." And now you toss both unfolded pieces of paper on the table (4). The audience will forget the order of the slips of paper and they will just see Wonder Woman and Superman and believe that you were right both times.

The most important part to make the One Ahead principle deceptive is that the audience doesn't see the paper as you take it out. Be sure to keep it hidden in your hands as you read it, but don't look like you are suspiciously hiding it because, at the end of the trick, you are very open and show the audience both pieces of paper together.

4

SUPERMAN

WONDER WOMAN

COIN to SHOE

Sometimes you just want to be able to make something disappear as if by magic. The Coin to Shoe is a great trick that can be either impressive or a very funny gag at a party.

You ask to borrow a quarter from someone in the room. As the person hands you that quarter, you clumsily miss the quarter and drop it to the floor (1). But when you pick it up, instantly the coin disappears. Now you can leave it completely vanished or, if you would like, you can reveal that the coin has traveled magically underneath your shoe.

Sometimes when I perform this, it is more of a gag where I pick the coin up, make it disappear, and then I say, "I never picked it up." And I then reveal that the coin is under my shoe. Because that is the secret to the trick: You will always be ready to do this amazing coin vanish because after you have "accidentally" dropped the coin, you bend over, and in looking like you are picking up the coin, you are actually sliding it under the front of your right shoe (2, 3).

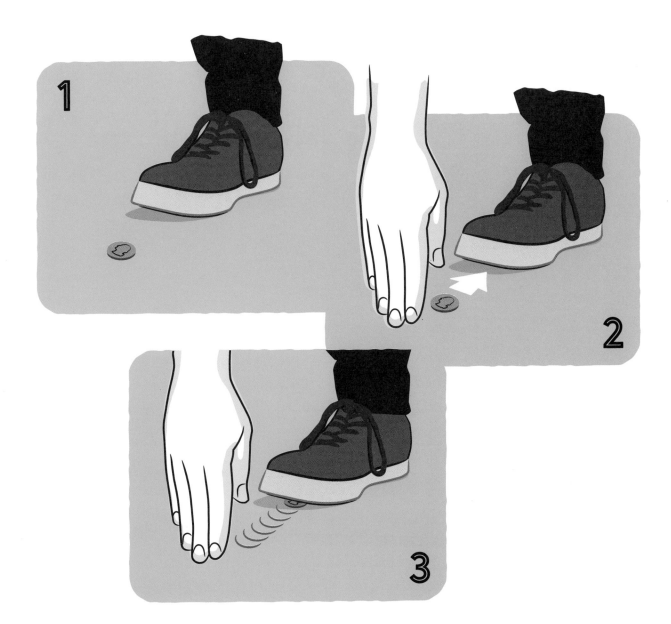

Now the coin is hidden under you shoe and you come up pretending that you are holding the coin. You take just a little bit of a moment for time misdirection and make the coin look as though it vanishes, when actually it is under your shoe the whole time.

Now you can choose to reveal it under your shoe like that is the magic trick or you can say, "I never picked it up." And reveal that the quarter is still on the ground by your shoe. Either way, it is a fun trick that gets a lot of reactions and one that I even performed in my professional show recently.

HAIR TIE *Switch*

Harry Houdini, one of the most famous magicians of all time, performed a trick called Metamorphosis, where two people would switch places in the blink of an eye. We are going to do a metamorphosis trick but this one is at your fingertips using a couple of hair ties.

In reality, these hair ties you'll use are actually craft loops or looms. They can be picked up at any craft store or department store, but I tell the spectator that they are hair ties because then they are seen as more familiar and ordinary objects. You have two different-colored hair ties. For the example, I am using white and gray. Drape the white loop over the gray loop (1) and fold the gray in half (2), creating a smaller hole. That is where you will rest the spectator's index finger and thumb.

Say, "Give me your index finger and thumb. I'm going to put the gray hair tie around it and then close your fingers so that they can't switch places." Now hold the white hair tie tight so they can see that the gray hair tie is locked around their thumb (3). You explain that Houdini used to switch places with someone in an instant and here, on your fingertips, we are going to make these two hair ties switch places in an instant, too.

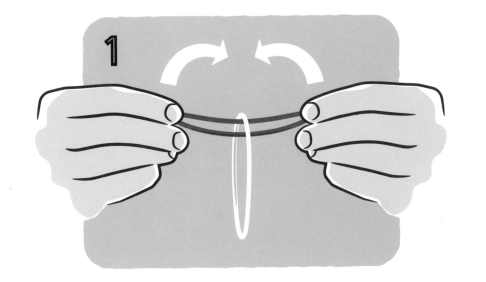

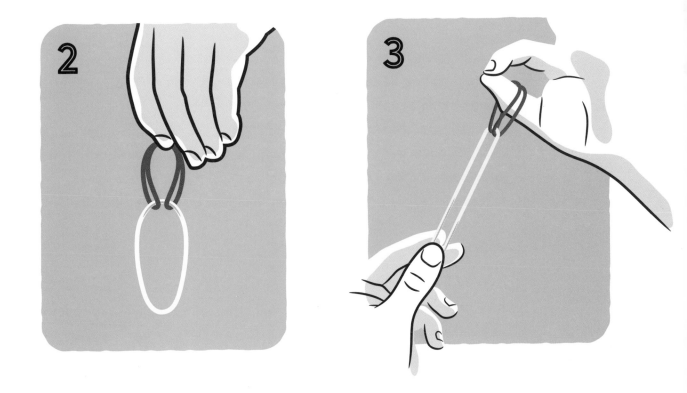

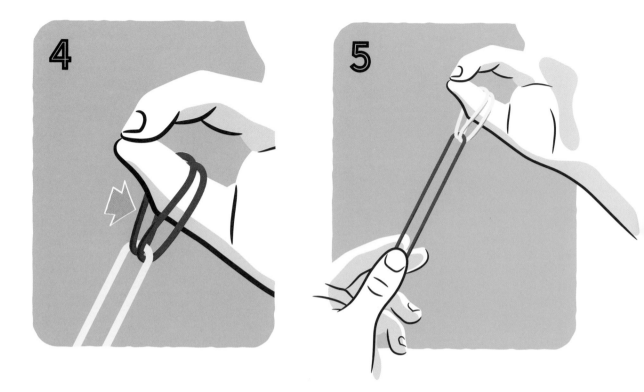

To make the magic happen, all you have to do is grab one side of the gray hair tie and pull (4). Be very careful to only grab one strand of the hair tie, but when you pull, the magic will happen automatically and the hair ties will switch. When you grab the gray hair ties, pull down in a swift, quick motion, and the magic will happen in an instant (5). You won't believe it by just reading this. You have to try it! It seems like an impossible switch because the audience believes the loops are locked in different positions. In reality, the loops can switch with each other with just a tug. Physics!

This is one of those cool things that you will perform for your friends again and again, but you will also love performing for yourself in the mirror because it looks so incredible. It is metamorphosis hair ties—magic in the blink of an eye.

Hot Rod FORCE

What if you want to force an audience to make a decision, but you don't want to do a card trick? Well, then you can use what magicians call the Hot Rod Force. This is an old principle in magic where you can get the audience to land on the color or item that you want by counting. You will provide a selection of one to six items. Your audience will choose a number one to six and they will always land on the right item, no matter what.

For example, let's say you have six different colors of Life Savers Gummies. You line them up in a row and the audience chooses any number (one to six) and you count that number to always arrive at the red Life Saver Gummy (1).

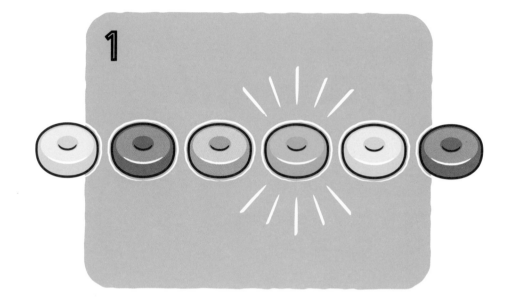

Here's how this trick works: If the audience selects the number one, you spell from the left to the right, O-N-E, and you land on the third Life Saver Gummy, which is your forced red Life Saver. If the audience says two, you spell T-W-O and land on the red Life Saver Gummy as well. If they say three, you count one-two-three to land on the red Life Saver Gummy. If the audience says four, you count to four from the opposite side (from the right to the left), so it is correct by their perspective (one-two-three-four) and you land on the red Life Saver Gummy. If the audience says five, you spell F-I-V-E to get to the red Life Saver Gummy. If the audience says six, then you go back to the other side and spell S-I-X to the red Life Saver Gummy. Each of those will give you the opportunity to force the red Life Saver Gummy on your friend.

Now why do you want to force a red Life Saver Gummy to be the chosen one in this trick? That's because it will lead you into the next amazing trick: the Gummy Stab.

the GUMMY STAB

For this trick, an audience member will select any Life Saver Gummy they want using the Hot Rod Force you just learned, and you are going to have the crazy ability to throw it in the air and stab your finger right through the hole of the Life Saver Gummy. Your friends will think you have a black belt in karate chops with how you are able to stab through the gummy with master precision.

Here's the secret: You already have the right Life Saver Gummy color wrapped around your first finger (1). But the audience doesn't see that because that hand is down at your side making a fist. You force the color of the Life Saver Gummy (in the previous trick, the Life Saver is red), you grab that color, and you throw it in the air. As you come to stab at it, you are actually catching it with your palm facedown in a forward motion. With a little bit of practice, you will be able to make it look like you throw the gummy in the air and stab it with your finger, when in actuality, you have caught it and you are hiding the extra gummy in your palm in your closed fist as your first finger reveals a "stabbed" Life Saver Gummy around your first finger.

This will make it look like you have crazy candy ninja skills!

How to
FORCE A CARD
(CUT FORCE)

This will be one of the most valuable lessons learned on your new magical journey and will help you with many tricks you might choose to perform down the road. You will be able to make anybody pick exactly the card that you want out of a deck of cards. As I mentioned in trick #21, we magicians call this a force, and this is my favorite force of a card in magic. It has been around for many, many years, and is called the Cut Force. You will know exactly where the audience cuts the deck, and you will be able to use this in the next two tricks in the book! In fact, this force can be used in any trick that requires your friend to pick a special card.

Here's how it works: You take the card that you would like to force and put it on the bottom of the deck. If you look at the picture, you will see what you are about to force: the five of diamonds. With the five of diamonds on the bottom of the deck, you are ready to perform this card force.

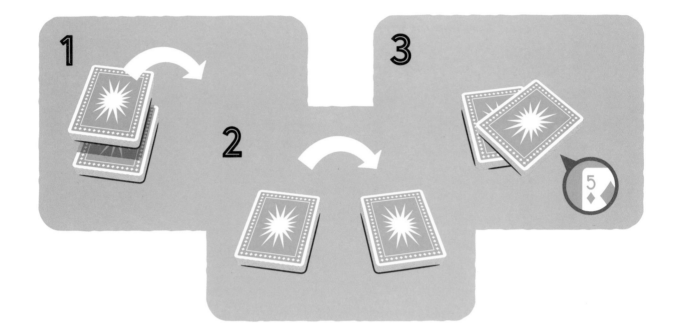

Tell your audience member to pick up half of the cards or wherever they like and set them on a spot on the table that you've pointed out (1, 2). The spot should be just a few inches away from the deck. Now you will pick up the rest of the cards and place them on top of the deck. However, as you do so, you are going to rotate the cards at a forty-five-degree angle and you are going to place them back on the deck (3). If you would like, you can even say, "I am going to complete the cut, but I'm going to leave it a little offset." (It is not important to say this, but if you would like to, you can.)

What you have done now is you have set up the trick so that after a little time misdirection, the audience will forget where the deck was cut. You will reveal the bottom card, but the audience will swear that that is where they cut the card. This is such a convincing magic trick that when I teach people, they even fool themselves. Really!

So, let's review: The audience member has cut the cards and you have replaced the bottom half of the deck on top, now sitting the cards at a forty-five-degree angle. You need what is called time misdirection. You explain to the audience member what is about to happen. This only has to take about 10 seconds, as that's the amount of time generally needed for "time misdirection." Time misdirection is something magicians use when we want an audience to forget a tiny detail. In this case, it's which half of the deck is on top and which is on bottom. I fill this moment by telling the audience what's about to happen next in the trick, then I go back to the deck.

Now you say, "Let's see what card you cut at." And you pick up the top half of the deck that you placed at a forty-five-degree angle and show them the card that supposedly they cut to, when in actuality that is your force card, the five of diamonds (4). It is a very convincing force when done well—and one that professional magicians still use to this day.

Here is something interesting and helpful to note: if you prefer, you can start with the force card on the top of the deck and then do the same actions as described above. The audience member cuts the cards and you place the bottom half on top of the deck at a forty-five-degree angle. Now after time misdirection, when you come back to the deck, you lift up the top half and you point to the facedown card on the bottom half of the deck, which is actually your force card. You say, "I can't see that card, but I want you to take a look at the card that you cut to." And when they do, they will be looking at your force card.

Pretty amazing, right? Well, the following trick will teach you some magic that you can do with this card force technique that you've just learned.

GHOST WRITING BILLS

Now that you have this new skill of making your friends choose whatever card you want, let's use that skill in this next trick to make a card mysteriously ghost-write onto your money. This is called Ghost Writer Bills, and this trick makes a card appear in ink on a dollar bill from nowhere, like a ghost writer.

In order to do this, you need two one-dollar bills. Prepare one of the dollar bills by writing the five of diamonds (or whatever force card you want to use) on the pyramid on the back of one of your bills. Make sure you don't write too hard, though, so that it bleeds through the front of the bill (1). You only want this visible when you are looking at the back of the dollar bill. Now take your other dollar bill and put it on top of that bill, so you can't see the writing. You can now get ready to perform this trick.

1

Holding both dollar bills in your hands with George Washington's face facing you, you are going to apparently show the back and front of both bills when actually concealing your secret writing.

Here's how you do it: Start holding on to the dollar bills with both hands with Washington's face toward you. Show the audience the face side of the top bill first and then rotate to show them the back of the bottom dollar bill by turning your wrists up. Now bring your wrists back down and peal the top bill off the face and put it down on the table. Immediately after dropping that dollar bill on the table, you bring your wrists back up, showing the back of the dollar bill still in your hand and bring it back down. To the audience, it will appear as though you have casually shown the front and back of both dollar bills when in actuality you showed the back of the bottom dollar bill twice. This is a classic magic move called the Flushstration Count.

Now to do the trick: You pick up both dollar bills and arrange them so that your bill with the writing is on top with George Washington facing you. You turn both bills facedown, and rotate the bill with no writing on it at a forty-five-degree angle so that the corners of both bills match up (2). But the writing will still be concealed underneath that bill.

Now you say, "We are going to see if we can make some writing appear on this dollar bill." You are going to roll up the bills next to better hide the ghost writing process. As you roll up the bill (3), the bill on the left (which is the bill that has the secret writing on it) will flip around to the top of the roll. Let that happen, but do not let the bill on the right flip around. As you do this, a weird thing happens where the rolling switches the orientation of the bills so that the bill with the writing on it is now on top. The audience will forget which dollar bill was on top and it will look as though the writing has just mysteriously appeared (4).

If you would like, you can have the audience put their fingers on the corners of both dollar bills as you see in the picture below. That not only helps keep the bills from rolling back up during the reveal, but is also a great way for your audience to participate in the magic.

ONE in a MILLION

Sometimes random events can align in a way that is truly magical—and almost impossible—like winning the lottery. For this trick, you are going to utilize some numbers, not much unlike lottery numbers, to make a crazy coincidence happen using a couple of borrowed objects.

Here's what your friends will see: They are going to give you a dollar bill, you crumple it up and protect it "from any sleight of hand by covering it with this handkerchief." They will then cut the deck of cards to a random spot in the deck, and remove the next eight cards. When all is revealed, impossibly the eight cards cut from the deck match the digits of the serial number of their dollar bill exactly! You remind them, "You could have given me any dollar bill and cut the deck anywhere, yet you cut to eight number cards that match, even in order, the serial number on your bill." It is the craziest coincidence you can do with a deck of cards and a dollar bill.

Here is how it is done: You are going to switch the dollar bill in one of my favorite ways: you can switch money using a hand-kerchief and a secret move. This is a really easy trick that you can master in seconds. It also uses the Cut Force you just learned!

Here's how you set up the trick: First, you need a regular dollar bill and you need to make note of its serial number. As an example, you have a dollar bill with a serial number of 15865744, so you'll gather an ace, a five, an eight, a six, five, seven, four, and four from the deck of cards (1). Put those cards in order on top of the deck. Crumple up your special known serial dollar bill and keep it palmed in your hand (2).

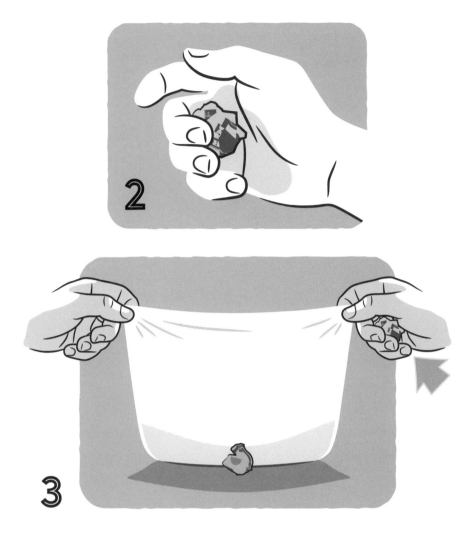

This is a special palm magicians call the *finger palm*. In your hand, the dollar bill is hidden behind the ring and pinkie finger. However, depending on the size of your hand, the dollar bill may be hidden behind all of your fingers. It's important to keep it naturally in a curled hand, held in your fingers. Now you are ready to perform the trick.

You borrow a dollar bill from your friend and have them crumple it up into a ball and place it on the table. You bring out a cloth napkin, bandanna, or handkerchief and you cover up that dollar bill because you are going to protect it so that nobody else can touch it (3).

Now you bring out your deck of cards and have your friend cut the cards somewhere in the middle of the deck. (This is when you execute what you learned in **How to Force a Card.**) Remember that you have the serial number order already in the playing cards on top of the deck and you are also going to do the Cut Force to make sure you get the numbers you want. Ask your friend to pick up about half the cards, place them next to it, and you replace the top half of the deck on those cards but at about a forty-five-degree angle. Then you say, "We'll come back to that." Remember in the last trick when I talked about time misdirection? It's the moment you explain what will happen next so the audience forgets the tiny detail in How to Force a Card (Cut Force).

Next, go to the bandanna and say, "Let's look at something interesting on your dollar bill." You pick up the bandanna from its center and the dollar bill underneath, and you will not let go of those again. Instead, you are going to let go of the hidden dollar bill in your finger palm and you release it as you lift up the bandanna (4). When that happens in sync, it appears as though your hidden dollar bill comes right from underneath the bandanna. It's a beautiful switch, and as long as you do it naturally while talking about what is going to happen next, the audience won't even think about it because, to them, the trick has hardly started yet. (In fact, nothing has happened yet, but the work is already done on your end! You are so far ahead of the game, you can sit back and relax.)

Ask your audience member to unroll the dropped dollar bill and to find the serial number. That serial number is going to match exactly where they cut the cards. Now, it's not that they cut the cards in the middle of the deck, but that you are instead taking the top half of the pack of cards and revealing what once was the top of the deck but is now the center of the cut force. Those cards *will* match the serial number exactly.

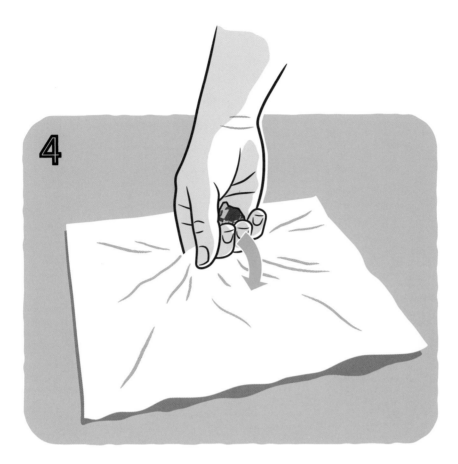

A couple important notes when choosing a dollar bill to use for this trick: 1) You want to find a serial number that you can replicate with playing cards. Sometimes it is difficult because a serial number might have a zero and you don't have a zero playing card. What I have done in those cases is use a queen because a Q is kind of like a zero, but if you can, you want to use a serial number that doesn't have any zeros, and 2) Try to choose a serial number that doesn't repeat any digit more than four times, as you'll only have four of each digit in one pack of cards.

That is one in a million, but if you want to use the secret code name, it is also called Serial Switch Cut Force.

Traveling MATCH

If you have ever wanted to make something disappear in a flash of fire, this trick is for you. In the Traveling Match, an ordinary match will vanish in a spark of fire and reappear hidden in a spectator's hands. In order to do this trick, you need an adult to get you a book of matches. These are paper matches folded into a little packet like a book. There are two different ways that you can set up this trick: one requires the help of an adult, and the other you can do by yourself. This is a trick that involves lighting a match. If you're a young magician, be sure to ask permission from an adult before you try the trick. Old magicians, you only have to ask permission if you want to.

The first way bends down a match from the center of the matchbook and separately lights it on fire and immediately burns it out. You just want to blacken one of those match heads. Make sure you or an adult can light it separately without starting the rest of the matches on fire. Once the lit match has cooled down, you place it back with the rest of the matches.

Or if you can't light a match ahead of time, you can just color in one of the match heads with black marker (1). Take one match head, bend it down, and color it in until it looks like it is completely burned. Now you are ready to perform the trick.

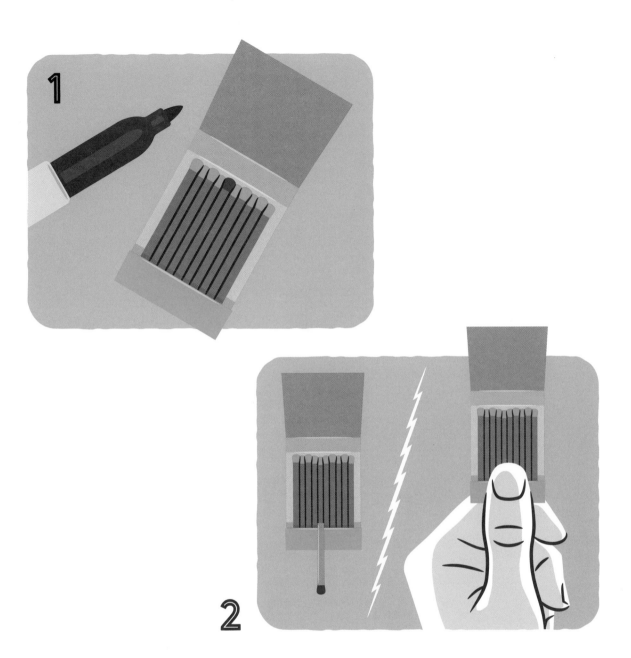

Once you have your friends in front of you, bring out the match book and, as you open it, fold your secretly prepared match down so that it's pointing to the floor. This is hidden behind your thumb (2). Show your friends the matchbook and make sure they see that all of the matches are unburned and brand new. Have your friend reach into the matches and take out any one that he likes, preferably somewhere near the middle.

Now, you are going to rotate the matchbook around your fingers, bringing the folded match head back into its regular position and closing the matchbook, all while being very careful to conceal that already burned/black match from your friends. You are now set to do a vanish-in-a-flash-of-fire move.

Have your friend hold the matchbook as you light the match against the matchbook (3). The match will vanish in a flash of fire and here's how: As you are shaking out the match, you throw that match to the floor. You just release it from your fingers and it will fall to the floor imperceptible to the audience because they are watching the flash of fire.

As soon as that match is dropped, do two more shakes and then pretend to place it in your opposite hand. This adds a little bit of misdirection so that when you slowly open your hand and the match is gone, the audience will have trouble imagining that you actually dropped the match on the floor.

Say something like, "I know it seems impossible, but in that flash of fire, the match has actually traveled back into the matchbook that you are holding on to." Then let your friend open the matchbook and they will go wild because not only is the burned match back in the matchbook, but it is reattached to the paper. They can tug on it and pull and see that it is really attached.

For a bonus effect, if you colored in the match with marker, you can relight that match by magic. You can say, "It is completely burned, but now I am going to make it relight." You strike that magic marker–colored match against the book, and it will relight like magic. This is such a cool trick, and your friends will completely be in awe.

DEAL Force

We're almost to the end of the book! But now the real fun begins. So far you've been learning everyday magic that happens in ordinary situations, but the last tricks I'm sharing can be performed in your first show! The tricks to follow can work in everyday situations, but I've also used them on stages around the world. (Of course, my first show was in my basement for all my neighborhood friends.) Wherever you decide to put on a show, these tricks will help you!

What I'm about to teach you is another way that you can make an audience member choose exactly what card you want. However, this audience member is going to swear that they mixed the cards and that at the last minute they had a free choice to change their mind (and that it was absolutely a free and random selection).

It's a very deceptive way of having your friend select a card. Once I teach it to you, you can make the outcome of the trick almost anything you want. You can make your friend's card appear on a ceiling fan that is spinning. You can make the card appear in your back pocket. You can even make the card appear in cryptic writing on your arm! We will get into that in the next trick. First, here is how to do an incredible card force on your friend. Magicians call it the Deal Force.

You are going to start with a deck of cards and two force cards on the top of the deck. These two cards should be different from one another in both number and suit (1), and both of them will be the force cards that you are going to make your friend select. Here's what I mean: You are going to have two outcomes to this trick. If your friend chooses the first card—say the four of clubs— then you are going to make the card appear on the ceiling fan (but the catch is, you will have already taped the four of clubs—a dupli- cate card—to the ceiling fan before the trick begins).

Then you'll need to choose a second force card—let's say the two of hearts. If your friend ends up with the two of hearts, you will take the trick in a different direction and maybe the two of hearts (again, a duplicate card) is already hidden in your back pocket or in a different room or maybe it is stuck to a clock—just somewhere that is an interesting reveal for the two of hearts. But how do we get your friend to make a selection between those two cards?

Here's the setup: You place the deck of cards facedown and you put the two force cards on top of the deck. Now, you can hand the deck of cards to your friend and tell them to deal cards into a pile one at a time, facedown. And they begin to deal the cards into a pile—one single pile—facedown. As they are dealing, you tell them that at any point they can stop dealing (2).

Once they have stopped dealing, you get rid of the remainder of the deck that is left in their hands and you say, "Great. Out of this pile we are going to now place the cards into two separate piles. So, deal one card right here," and point to your friend's left. "And put the next card here," and point to your friend's right. Then say, "Now, go back and forth dealing cards into these two piles, sorting the cards randomly into each pile."

Your friend will take the cards that they have just dealt and now basically separate them into two piles. Here is what you have done: You have taken the two force cards that were buried in the first initial deal and brought them back to the top of each respective pile (3). So, now you have a seemingly free choice at the end of this process for your friend.

Once the cards are all dealt out, tell your friend, "We have mixed the cards and you have dealt different piles here." And make it seem very random as you explain this. "Last thing, I'm going give a choice of either the right pile or the left pile and whichever one you choose, that's the one we are going to use. Ready? Choose." Let's say your friend chooses the pile on the right. You turn over the card, and they see the four of clubs. Now you have your force card, but you have an added level of deception. Now you can say, "Very good. Remember, you could have chosen the pile on the left." And then you reveal the other force card, the two of hearts.

You say, "It's some random card, the two of hearts." And you pretend as though that wasn't a perfectly acceptable outcome of the trick. Now with the four of clubs, you can reveal wherever you have the duplicate four of clubs hidden—the climactic revelation!

Many card tricks have many different revelations, whether they are secret writing appearing on cards or cards being put in interesting locations. This trick is a great starting point for you to learn how to create your own magic. You have an amazing method to start with where you can have your friend end up with one of two cards, even though it seems completely haphazard and random. With this method, you can create new magic routines that require your friend to select predetermined cards. Or you can proceed to the next trick and use the method in one of my favorite tricks to do in live shows when I perform for large audiences.

COFFEE STAIN

It's time for your first real show as a magician. So far, you have been learning magic that you can do in ordinary situations, like hanging out with your friends. But the last three tricks in this book are meant to be performed on small stages for audiences of your friends, family, and strangers. This is your big break!

The first trick perfectly suited to a larger audience is Coffee Stain. It is based on an old trick that used ashes, but I've given it a modern twist by using coffee grounds instead. That way I can carry this trick around in my pocket with a small packet of instant coffee. It is a wild trick that will seem as if you can make a playing card appear in eerie writing across your arm beneath some coffee grounds. Sound weird? It is, but it is also incredibly amazing!

Here's how you do it: First, you will need to have a card selected in a very fair way. This will actually be a Deal Force (see previous trick). You have two cards on the top of the deck that you know the hidden identity of. Let's say those cards are the six of hearts and the four of diamonds. You start with the six of hearts and the four of diamonds on top of the deck. You hand the deck of cards to someone out in the audience and say, "We are going to choose a card in the fairest way possible. Deal down cards into a single pile facedown and whenever you want to stop, you can stop dealing the cards."

Your audience member begins dealing cards into a single pile. They don't have to count. They don't have to keep track. They just keep going until they want to stop. Once they stop you say, "Do you want to stop right there? If you would like to, you can keep going or we can go back a little bit." Whatever your audience member decides is totally fine. Because now he hands those cards he just dealt to the person next to him, and that person is going to deal those cards into two new piles to make an even greater free choice. (This is what brings your "force cards" to the top of the two piles.)

After the cards are dealt into two piles, you tell the audience member that they get to choose whichever pile they want. The pile they choose is the pile you are going to use. They pick the pile on the left or the right. Once they have made a choice, the audience member reveals the card on top of that pile. It is either going to be the six of hearts or the four of diamonds. Even though it seems like they have made all of their own decisions, you predetermined and knew that they were going to select either the four of diamonds or the six of hearts.

Now that one of your deal force cards has been chosen, you can make that card appear on your arm with coffee grounds in a very eerie way (1).

The preparation for this trick requires just a little bit of ChapStick. That's right, ChapStick! You take a tube of Chap-Stick, but instead of putting it on your lips, you draw on your arm before performing your magic show (2). The audience won't be able to see it, but when the time comes, it will make for a very eerie illusion. On your right arm you draw the six of hearts, and on you left arm you draw the four of diamonds. The only thing you have to remember is which card is on which arm.

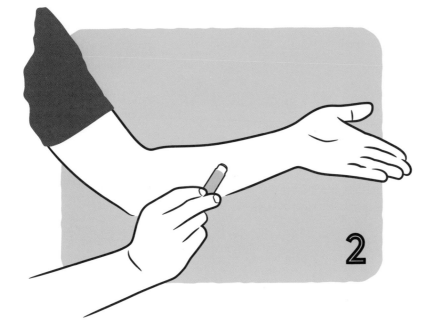

Now, when you perform the card force, the audience really does get a free choice of whichever pile they want, so it really feels like they ended up with a free choice of either the six of hearts or the four of diamonds.

After the card has been chosen, grab a little bit of coffee grounds to make the magic happen. Hold out the correct arm depending on which card the audience member chose. Now, rub a little bit of coffee grounds on your bare arm (3) and watch it stick to that ChapStick and reveal the eerie writing of the card that they chose (4). What a cool trick!

You can do some more with this as well with a little bit of research. Maybe instead of doing this as a card trick, you can make the initials of somebody's mom or dad appear on your arm. In order to do that, you just have to know the name of the person that they are going to think of.

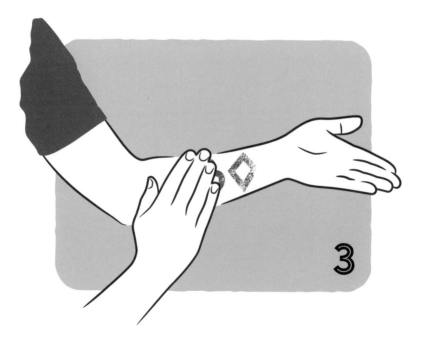

This trick is only limited by your creativity. I have done this trick with words appearing on my arm! I once made the whole word "unbelievable" appear on my arm because I knew that I could make a particular spectator think of the word *unbelievable*. But most often this trick is done very easily with a card force, ChapStick, and coffee grounds to create what looks like a truly magical illusion.

TRICK #29

ROPE TIE

A master magician can escape from anything he is tied up in, and I am going to show you exactly how. In fact, you are going to turn this into a true magic trick by making it appear as though you can escape from rope tied all around you in an instant (or it will appear that you can instantly make a jacket penetrate through the ropes onto your body). It is a crazy trick. Let me show you what it looks like.

To your audience, you'll look as though you are tied up by your friends. You will step behind a curtain that your friends hold up or hop inside of a coat closet, and when you emerge from the curtain or the coat closet, you will have on a jacket with the ropes still tied firmly around your body. This is a magic classic often called the Gypsy Rope Tie. Let me show you how it's done.

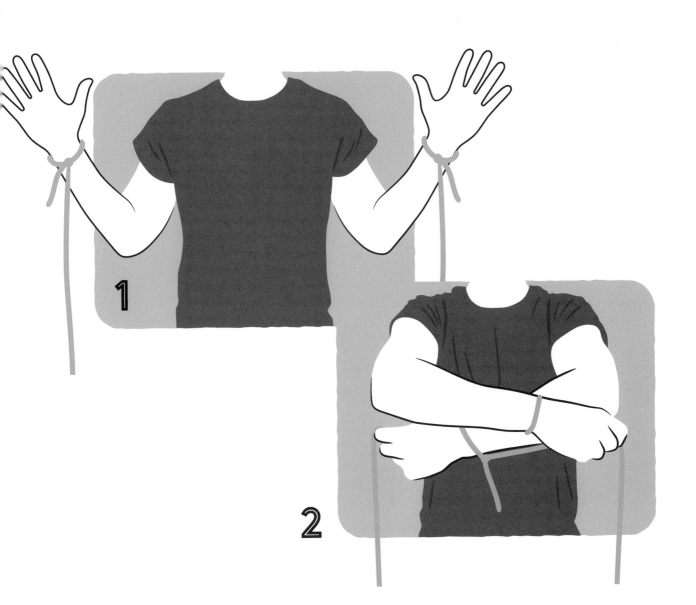

You need two pieces of rope each about ten feet in length. It is not special rope or magician's rope, so any rope from a hardware or home store will work just fine. You are going to instruct your friends to tie the ends of the rope around your wrists. Your friends can tie the rope around your wrists as tightly as they like, because it will stay put the entire time (1).

Once your left hand and your right hand are completely tied, you are going to make it appear as though the ropes will hold your arms to your body, kind of like a straightjacket (when in actuality, you will be completely free to open your arms).

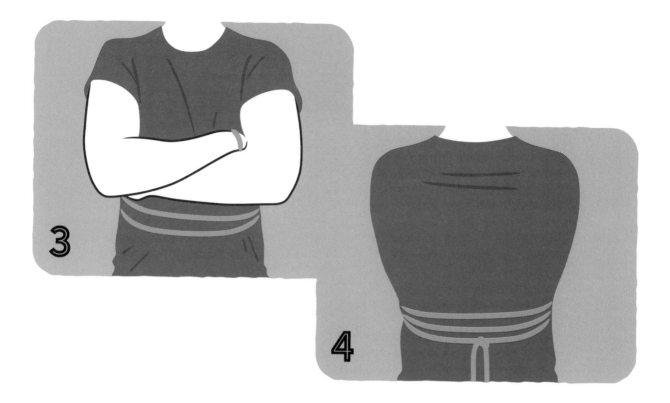

Here is how that is done: It should appear that you cross your arms and allow the spectators to grab the rope and pull your arms tight to your body. However, that is only the illusion. What actually happens is instead of the right hand taking the right piece of rope and the left hand the left piece of rope and passing that back, the right hand will grab the left hand's rope and the left hand will grab the right hand's rope (2). Then let those ropes slip through your fingers as you bring them around to the back. You do this in the action of turning your back toward the audience and crossing your arms (3).

Now your friends can pull as tightly as they want because when the knot is all tied (4), you will still be able to open your arms wide (5). This is the secret to being able to put on a jacket, even though you are completely tied up. So, everyone checks the knots on everything and you step into the coat closet or behind a big blanket that your friends hold up to conceal you.

Somebody tosses you a jacket and you are able to put on that jacket because you can open up your arms. Once the jacket is on, fold your arms again as though you are still tied tightly, and either have your friends drop the blanket or you step out of the coat closet. It will appear that the jacket has penetrated the ropes and you are now wearing it.

To take off the jacket, do the same in reverse. Step behind the large blanket or back into the coat closet so that you can take off the jacket and come back out still tied up. It is important with getting out of this trick at the end that you allow people to either cut you out or to untie the knots to keep the illusion that you really were tied up the entire time.

This is an incredible piece of magic that will make it appear as if you are either lightning fast or that the jacket magically passes through the ropes and the magician's arms without your moving. It is pretty amazing. You are going to want to practice putting the jacket on fast in the privacy of your own home before attempting this in front of an audience. Speed is a big factor in making this trick believable.

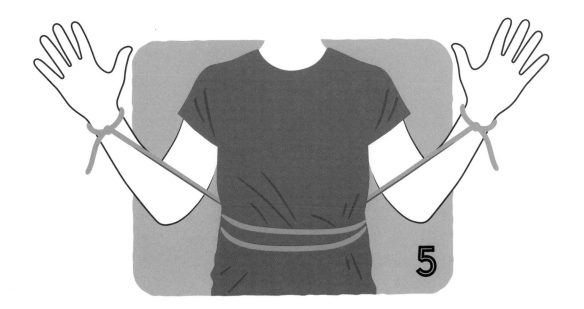

Also, it would be good to find a jacket that is bigger than your actual size. So, if you are a kid, get an adult's jacket. If the jacket is too small, it will be difficult to fold your arms once it's on.

Finally, when you initially put on the jacket, make sure your right and left hands are close to your body underneath the jacket to hide the fact that the rope is going in the opposite direction than it should. What you can do is have the audience check your wrists and your back to make sure that the rope is still tied securely. They do that by looking up the sleeves of the jacket you are now wearing and lifting up the back of the jacket to see the rope is tightly tied around the back.

CARD in the LEMON

I've saved the best for last. This is the granddaddy of all card tricks. This is the classic of magic that people will talk about for ages, and this is the perfect way to close your first magic show. Get ready because this is a miracle trick. Magicians call it the Card in the Lemon. It is an amazing piece of magic where anybody's selected card will end up sealed inside of God's creation—fruit perfectly sealed by nature. That's why it is so amazing. How can something get inside of a piece of fruit? Well, I'm going to teach you how right now.

The audience will see a card selected and then it will appear as though that card is inside of a lemon. It appears that way because it really is. Here is how you put a card in a lemon.

Grab a lemon and you will see that there are two ends. One end has a bump, but the other end has a pip, which is where the stem was. You want to find that pip and remove it (1). You can kind of massage it and it will fall out and it will leave a little divot. Save that pip because you are going to reuse it in a moment.

Now get a pencil, Sharpie, or a pen and very carefully poke directly into the lemon (2). As you get better and better at this, it will start to become imperceptible that you have poked into the fruit and there won't be any cracking around where the pip was. If the fruit does crack around that area, it is okay, because in a moment you are going to seal it up.

Next, take the card that you want to appear in the lemon and fold it up. If you are going to use the three of diamonds, later on that will be your force card. So fold the card in half widthwise and then roll it into a small little tube. The tighter you roll this, the easier it will be to put in the lemon (3).

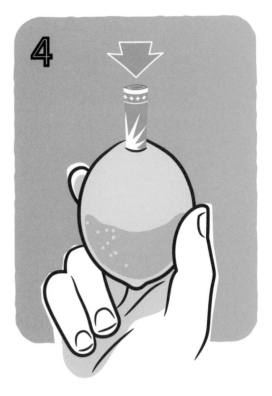

Then you go to the hole you just made with the pencil and slide that card right inside (4). You push it as far in as you can with your fingers and then grab your pencil and push it in so that it is about in the center. Now all you need is a little bit of Super Glue and that saved pip that you kept from earlier. Glue the pip back into place (5). And there—you have an ordinary-looking lemon that is ready to perform a miracle.

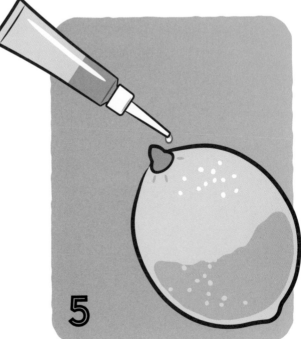

One tip is that you don't want to set up this lemon too early because right now the card is soaking up all sorts of lemon juices and it won't be able to last for much longer than an hour or so before it gets really soggy. If you would like, you can poke the hole in the lemon and then roll up a paper towel and put that inside. If you let the towel soak for an hour, it will absorb a lot of the juice before you put in the card. That's just an extra tip from somebody who has done the trick a hundred times himself.

Now that you are ready to perform the trick, you are going to choose one of the card forces you would like to do. My favorite to use is the Cut Force that you learned earlier.

Announce to the audience that you are going to make a card vanish and appear someplace impossible, someplace that nobody has ever seen before. And the reason nobody has ever seen it before is because it is inside something that was growing on a tree.

Have an adult, or if you would like to do so on your own very carefully, take the knife and start to cut around the edge of the lemon, right down the center. You don't want to cut all the way through because, if you cut all the way through, you will hit the playing card that is perpendicular to the knife.

Once you have cut around all the way, you can take both halves of the lemon in each of your hands, give it a little bit of a twist, and open it up. The audience will see something they have never seen before: A playing card is sticking out of half of a fruit (6). Even better, when they take it out and unroll it, it is not just any card; it is the card that they cut to moments earlier.

It's an amazing piece of magic—one that I think could close your first magic show and one that you will be performing for years to come. This trick is *so* good, it can be the grand finale of your first magic show. I love performing it and I know you will, too. Even better, if you have a pencil, a deck of cards, and a little bit of Super Glue, you will always be ready to do some magic with your friend's fruit.

HOW TO BECOME THE
ULTIMATE
MAGICIAN

Whew! Thirty tricks! I'm sure your
head is rattling with new moves and routines
you can't wait to try out on your friends.
But before I let you go, I want to share
a few more secrets. Ready?

How to Get Good

When I was a young magician, I received the incredible privilege of having breakfast with a real-life famous magician, Lance Burton. At the time, Lance was in the middle of a one-hundred-million-dollar Las Vegas show and was larger than life to me. Today, I'm lucky to call him a friend, but back then, as just a kid starting out, he became a sort of mentor by giving me a golden piece of wisdom that I now pass on to you. Ready?

You have to find your Hamburg.

What a second, you might be thinking. *What on earth does that mean?* To explain, you have to know the story of the Beatles. Sure, you may know the band and all about Beatlemania of the sixties and the massive hits that changed music forever, but did you know about the Beatles in Hamburg, Germany? Hamburg is where John, Paul, George, and Ringo where able to perform every night for hours each night at a local pub. The conditions weren't glamorous and the money was nonexistent, but they went onstage for months at a time, and after a thousand hours of playing together live, they became the group that we know as the Beatles.

As a young magician, the most important thing—even more important than what tricks you perform—is getting out there and doing it! You can't become a great magician without real-life performances in front of friends, family, and strangers. You see, magic only exists in the mind of a spectator. When practicing a trick's secret moves in front of a mirror, there's no magic—only sleights and finger flicking. It's when someone sees the sleight and experiences the deception that they experience wonder. Boom: you have magic!

Where was my Hamburg, you ask? I'm a slow learner so I had a couple. I grew up with a magician for a dad, and he'd teach me a new trick every month that I could then perform at the local magic club. That was before I was ten years old and one of those tricks, a trick with an egg, is still in my show today. As I grew older, I took every opportunity to perform. Church functions, county fair talent shows, birthday parties—anywhere I was allowed to do my tricks. Eventually, I had my thousand hours and started to get paid to do magic, a whopping twenty-five bucks a show!

I've had quite a journey. From county fairs to Madison Square Garden, magic has taken me around the world. After putting in the years of work, my magic was discovered by Ellen DeGeneres, which then helped put me onstage in Madison Square Garden, and now more than one billion people watch my magic online and on television. I still tour with my live show, and I love to create new tricks every day.

I'm astonished by what magic has made possible. That's why I'll always continue to make magic and share joy!

How to Dress Like a Magician

When I was eight years old, I wanted to dress up like a magician for Halloween. What do you think I wore? A top hat and tuxedo, of course! Do you know why the top hat and tuxedo has forever remained synonymous with magicians? It all started with a French magician named Jean-Eugène Robert-Houdin, who was the father of modern magic because he took the magician out of wizard ropes and away from magic spells and into the outfit of a gentleman of that era—a tuxedo. That was all the way back in the 1800s! Well, every other magician followed suit, including an English magician who would be the first to pull a rabbit from a borrowed top hat: David Devant.

These two magicians influenced the art of performing magic more than any other person before and perhaps more than any since. It's important to realize that the reason Robert-Houdin and Devant used tuxes and top hats was because that was the formal clothing of their time. I'm convinced that if everyone was wearing jeans and baseball hats in the 1800s, then Robert-Houdin would have worn jeans onstage and David Devant would have pulled a furry animal from a borrowed baseball hat.

I share this with you only so you know that you don't have to wear a top hat and a tux to be a magician. In fact, your magic will likely be more surprising if you dress in ordinary clothes. It's the reason this book is titled *Everyday Magic for Kids*, because I want you to be a magician *every day* in *ordinary situations*.

Make Magic, Share Joy

I spent many hours deciding what magic to teach you in these pages. I asked trusted magician friends and even worked with my team of creators to bring brand-new tricks to you. Some of these tricks will follow you for the rest of your life. I can't tell you the amount of times I've made salt vanish, matches travel, or rubber bands jump just because the ingredients happened to be at the table. And that's when the magic is most organic—when it's unprepared. To be honest, those moments are often more powerful to the spectator because the magic seems to come from nowhere! That's when you hear surprised and stunned people say, "The magician just grabbed my dollar and did magic! He didn't have special props or anything!"

Memorize the following tricks, practice hard, and they'll serve you well. You may find a new confidence when talking to strangers or maybe you'll build a small community of magicians with your friends and neighbors. Whatever the outcome, enjoy the journey and constantly be searching for new secrets to master. I love the pursuit of wonder because it never ends. And I hope you get to experience that joy as well through the art of magic.

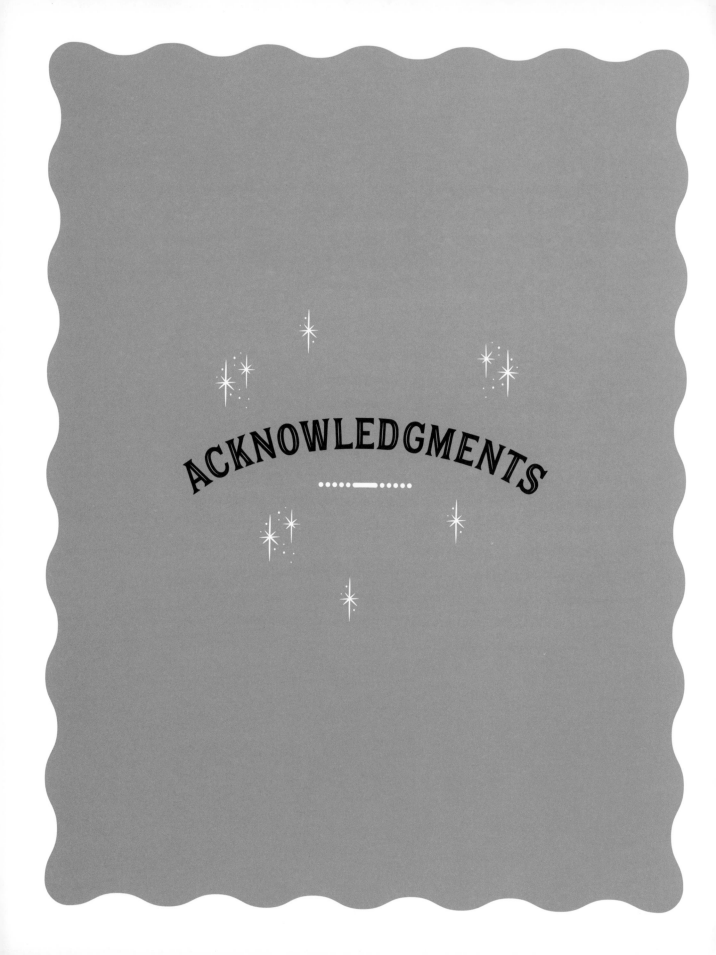

ACKNOWLEDGMENTS

This book was a blast to write and really took me back to when I was a kid reading magic books that I borrowed from the public library or old books from my dad's shelf. Most of the secrets in this book are classics in magic and some a century old. I've updated some of the props and presentations but rarely is a new concept invented in magic. Therefore, I must thank the magicians who came before me who made this magic possible, most notably Mark Wilson, whose *Complete Course in Magic* has been a solid guide to learning the basics of magic since 1975.

Darryl Davis and Daryl Williams (a.k.a., the Other Brothers) sat with me for hours playing with new and old magic tricks. We took a list of a hundred and slowly edited it to the thirty in this book. I'm very thankful for their insight and creativity in choosing and updating these classics.

Tyler Erickson was my first formal magic teacher. He took my passion and molded it into a discipline and an understanding of the art of magic. It's his wisdom that guided the choices for the best tricks to include in this book.

My circle of friends in Las Vegas has proven to be the most valuable group of individuals who teach me something new about magic every time we collaborate. These are magicians like Bizzaro, Ryan Stock and AmberLynn, Patrick Kun, Kyle Marlett, Kyle and Mistie Knight, Greg Dow, Shimshi, Nick Diffatte, Amazing Johnathan, Shawn Farquhar, Justin Willman, Josh Jay, Calen Morelli, Johnny Thompson, Greg Wilson, Nate Staniforth, James Galea, Dan White and Blake Vogt, Tim Trono, Doug McKenzie, Jeff McBride, and many more too numerous to name.

Rick Lax is my closest advisor, creator, and friend. We've collaborated on television shows, viral videos, and original magic tricks. Our friendship has radically affected my magic thinking, and he continues to encourage my development as a performer.

ABOUT THE AUTHOR

Minnesota born, Justin Flom has built a magical life. From touring with Country Superstars Florida Georgia Line and creating magic for Coca-Cola's international ad campaign, Justin truly has the ability to entertain anyone, anywhere!

Whether appearing on *Ellen*, the *Today Show*, *Rachael Ray*, or network late-night shows, with WWE Wrestling stars or on his own show for two seasons on Syfy, *Wizard Wars*, Flom has astonished more than a billion people worldwide.

After graduating from high school and spending a few years in Branson, Missouri, entertaining audiences, Justin began posting magic videos on YouTube, Instagram, Facebook, and anywhere else he could find an outlet online. The efforts paid off when the staff of *Las Vegas Weekly* named him Best Up-And-Coming Entertainer of the Year in 2013. But Justin's proudest accomplishment is his incredibly happy marriage with Jocelynn and the birth of their first child, daughter Haven! At just four months old, Haven starred in her first video by being "cut" in half by her dad. The video has been seen by more than one hundred million people online.

Justin Flom continues to captivate both online and in person. His fan number grows exponentially every week. He is thankful daily for a family who planted a seed to entertain, to make people laugh and smile, and to sometimes gasp, and he looks forward to gathering in a new generation of magic lovers.

Make Up Your Own Tricks!

Write or draw them here

Make Up Your Own Tricks!

Write or draw them here

Make Up Your Own Tricks!

Write or draw them here